To Dylan,

MOTIVATING KIDS TO THE MAX

May you have a very successful future

Richard O'Connell

3/31/09

RICHARD
O'CONNELL, ED. D.

Visit www.booksurge.com to order additional copies.

MOTIVATING KIDS TO THE MAX

For Parents, Counselors, Teachers, Administrators, Guidance Secretaries and Interns

2006

COVER PICTURE

The cover picture is meant to symbolize the **DIVERSE NATURE** of the counselor's caseload and the **REQUIRED SKILLS** needed to **MOTIVATE KIDS TO THE MAX.**

On the left is the "Kende Trio," representing academic achievement at a local high school and long years of sacrifice traveling into New York City every Saturday to attend the famed Juilliard School of Music, culminating in acceptance to Princeton University for all three girls. (See Addendum 12 for more information.)

On the right are new **ENGLISH LANGUAGE LEARNERS** with their teacher at an evening function sponsored by the guidance department to welcome new ELL students and their families into the school community. (See Chapter 7 for more information.)

The bright color green was chosen purposefully as a background, since **GREEN** symbolizes new life and the principal message counselors must give their students...**HOPE!**

(Cover by Paul Caravelli, A **"CAN DO ALL"** PRODUCTION
pcaravelli@earthlink.net)

CONTENTS

PART ONE

MOTIVATIONAL GUIDANCE AND THE SCHOOL COMMUNITY

CHAPTERS

PART TWO

THE MECHANICS OF MOTIVATIONAL GUIDANCE

MOTIVATING KIDS TO THE MAX

There are many aspects to this book which are unorthodox, one of which is to begin with a book review. It is placed here for two reasons: for those who wish to learn more about the book and for those who will enjoy a well-written review that is not over the top with sensationalism.

BOOK REVIEW
By Lisa Di Benedetto (Parent and Former Corporate Media Specialist)

"MOTIVATING KIDS TO THE MAX" is truly the quintessential guide to guidance. Do not be fooled by the title, which humbly claims merely to improve guidance services. What the author does is to re-invent, clarify, humanize and add life to the previously mundane task of motivating students. The book is a quick read further enhanced by the many anecdotes that provide real-life applications for the many insights so useful to parent and counselor alike.

The author's approach is an artful combination of diplomacy, humor and decades of experience in the real world of guiding young people to achieve their full potential. It is a step-by-step guide for how counselors, administrators, teachers and parents can pull together for the benefit of the student. Dr. O'Connell has effectively identified the rough spots (that typically have to do with ego or lack of experience) that can easily derail what should be a harmonious team effort within the school system in the student's behalf. The many awards earned for superior guidance skills are reflected in the author's understanding of human nature and willingness to adjust, fine tune or even reverse his approach when warranted.

As a public relations professional specializing in training corporate chief executive officers to deal with confrontational media interviews, I recognized many of the same techniques in Dr. O'Connell's approach to preparing students for college interviews. The author's success as a guidance counselor is clearly built upon a powerfully refined and intuitive sense about people including students, parents, college admissions officers and the entire extended school community. These same people skills are artfully applied to identifying and developing his students' natural talents and promoting these strengths to college universities or vocational situations.

As the mother of four (three already in college), the book provided insights I had not previously considered and which will surely prove valuable when my fourth child applies to college. Clearly, Dr. O'Connell's approach leaves no student behind from the most learning disabled to the most gifted. His anecdotes about foreign students and his work helping them to mainstream into the school community demonstrate that every student has something important to contribute to the school. The author is equally skilled at guiding highly gifted students to the best schools in the nation.

"MOTIVATING KIDS TO THE MAX" was a quick and joyful read, illuminating and delightful in every way. It should become a reference book for guidance counselors nationwide and it is a must-read for parents and other school personnel who desire to guide and assist their children and students in achieving their full potential.

ACKNOWLEDGEMENTS

A MOST SINCERE WORD OF THANKS

1. To my dedicated secretaries: Georgette Bogdanowich, Jo Ann Morley and Janice Cassone with whom I have worked for seventeen years. Their generosity to me and to students is immeasurable; their concern and kindness helped to create a family setting for students.

2. To Joyce Kechian, Kathy Rose and Kathleen Tisch, for their patience and persistence in translating my hieroglyphic notes into understandable English

3. To Ruth Newland for ten years of previous secretarial service; she exemplified all that a counselor could ask for in a guidance secretary and human being.

4. To my interns: Jonathan Way, Susan Fedora and Joel Fernandez whose burden it was to take down my counseling advice and transcribe it into readable English

5. To April Ryan, a high school clerical assistant, whose virtues are best exemplified in Chapter 2, paragraph 1, "Heroic Students"

6. To Byrn Tomanek, who on other collaborative projects exemplified the true and generous involvement of a concerned parent

7. To Paul Caravelli for his exceptional photographic and technical skills

8. To Bob Emery (Director of Guidance), Faith Keenan (Guidance Counselor), Colette Patak (Learning Disability Specialist), Matthew Bonora (Board of Education Member) and, Dr. John Kehoe (Assistant Superintendent of Schools) for their friendship and professional input

9. To Christina, David, Thomas, Henry, Michael, Richard, Laura and Janice for their inspiration and my many friends who contributed in the search for meaningful quotations to augment the text.

10. And especially to Lisa Kende whose friendship, erudition and editorial skills were exceptional.

Dedication

This Handbook Is Dedicated
To All My Former Students
And Educational Colleagues
With Whom I Have Had The Privilege Of Working,

And To My Wife, Kathleen
And My Son, Peter
With Whom I Have Had The Joy And Privilege Of Living!

HOW TO MOTIVATE STUDENTS

In order to motivate kids to the max, all aspects of a student's school and personal life must be considered. All avenues of approach must be utilized. This book deals with the student's adolescent/pre-adolescent years and it is the people in the school community (parents, teachers, counselors, administrators and guidance interns) who, in one form or another, have the opportunity to motivate.

Motivation is multifaceted and takes different shapes, forms and combinations of people.

It depends on the academic, emotional, behavioral, and social factors that so powerfully affect a youngster's performance. No one person by him/herself can necessarily bring about change. It is sharing and working together as a team that really changes kids. However, there is one person in the school who is in uniquely positioned to address all these issues, in conjunction with parents, teachers and administrators, and that is the school counselor.

The reader is asked to take and use the advice given to the counselor in this book as if it was given to him or her and to view the word guidance more in terms of motivation than giving direction.

The reader should consider each topic in the context of his/her particular circumstance and needs. Also, consider any advice given to school personnel on motivating, organizational skills, teacher relations, technical matters, etc. according to his/her role in helping students. The book shares many decades of experience on how parents, teachers and administrators, working together and in conjunction with the school counselor, can be the most effective way in MOTIVATING KIDS TO THE MAX.

As a counselor for over forty years, I knew it was time to retire when one of my newly transferred, twelfth grade Hispanic students sought my advice. I spent a great deal of time with her on her personal problems and strategizing to help her graduate from high school. A few weeks later, she came back to me and I asked, "How are you doing and how do you like your new school?" Her eyes lit up and she said, "Oh! Dr. O'Connell, I am doing fine. I made new friends and my teachers are so nice. They are like my **MOTHER and FATHER**...and you, you Dr. O'Connell, are just like my...........**GRANDFATHER**." It is funny how we never consider ourselves aging, but in the eyes of teenagers, anyone over 25 is old.

Now that I am retired, I thought that I would leave a legacy of best practices based on my successes and failures. The guidance profession is one that is open to extreme accountability and for counselors it can be a minefield of explosive situations. What better gift could I give the school community (students, parents, counselors, administrators, teachers, guidance secretaries, and interns) than to share with young and veteran counselors and all those who work with them, a lifetime of experiences in guidance? As a battle scarred veteran, my advice is all I have to give.

My work is a compendium of strategies, approaches, organizational skills, time savers, motivational techniques, etc. It ranges: **from** advice on how to improve teacher, administrative and parental relations, to enhancing student accountability **from** motivational strategies for struggling students, to following administrative directives, **from** dealing with troublesome parents, to helping college bound and learning disabled students, etc.

I am hoping that this handbook will give counselors, administrators, teachers, secretaries, and parents the knowledge and wisdom that took **GRANDFATHER** so long to learn.

The format of this handbook is to present various guidance topics.

In the handbook will be what I regard as significant advice or approaches to each topic. It is divided into two sections, which deal with motivating students, Motivational Guidance and the School Community and the Mechanics of Motivational Guidance. **I do not claim to exhaust each topic.** The handbook assumes that the reader will have a general knowledge of the area addressed. The handbook was written for the high school and middle school communities.

It has application as well for parents whose children will soon be entering middle school. Part of the usefulness of this handbook is that middle school parents will also gain a greater insight into the mechanics and nature of guidance services in the senior high school.

By the way, the young Hispanic girl did solve most of her personal problems and did graduate from high school.

ABOUT THE TITLE

There were a number of titles which could have applied to this handbook. Its principal orientation is practices that enhance guidance services which for purposes of this book are syonymous with motivating students. In compiling the handbook, I wanted to impress upon the reader that guidance services are really delivered through the collective efforts of the school community. Each reader can gain significant insights into his/her role in delivering guidance services. Each can apply its concepts to the improvement of services in his/her area. Multiple topics have pertinence to each member of the school community throughout the handbook. Before I chose the present title, I struggled with different titles to incorporate the concept of guidance as a school community approach rather than the sole responsibility of the guidance department. Some were very serious, others comical.

The first title I chose was:

"Guidance for Dummies"

Besides being possibly copyrighted, this title really belied and maligned the counselor,who has to be:

Part psychiatrist:
Part psychometrician (the psychological theory of mental measurement)
Part social worker
Part mental health expert
Part Noble Prize Peace Candidate
Part occupational and career specialist
Part academic savant and, regrettably, at times, a "babysitter"
Part New York State (your state) regulations specialist
Part grieving student specialist

Part surrogate parent
Part attorney and legal expert
Part drug counselor
Omniscient college expert
Omniscient motivational expert
Omniscient record keeper
A "Jack of All Trades"
(See Addendum 1. for examples of the multiple duties of a counselor.)

A second comical title was considered:

"Improving Guidance Services Based on a Lifetime of Mistakes."

I discarded this title because it would be a three volume series.

Then I considered:

**"All You Wanted to Know about Middle and Senior High
School Guidance but Were Afraid to Ask"**

This title conveyed the notion of a mystique and fear, which should not exist.

Or

"The Inner Workings of the Guidance Department"

This was a good title and the handbook does convey the inner workings but the title lacks the concept of improvement through a united school effort.

Or

"What Goes on Behind the Counselor's Closed Door?"

This title conveys the notion of absolute privacy and secrecy, when

80% of the time, it is just everyday business. Besides, a counselor's door should always be open, **for obvious reasons**, except when privacy is absolutely necessary.

Or

"Best Practices for Middle and High School Guidance Counselors"

This was the original title, but did not include administrators, teachers, secretaries, interns, and parents as contributing to improving motivational guidance services.

I finally chose:

MOTIVATING KIDS
TO THE MAX

A Practical and Candid Handbook
For
Parents, Counselors, Teachers, Administrators,
Guidance Secretaries and Interns

With special reference to:
ASPIRING IVY LEAGUE students,
LEARNING DISABLED students,
UNMOTIVATED students
FOREIGN BORN and AVERAGE students

This lengthy title was selected in the **hope** that it will help the school community gain greater insights into guidance services.

As a counselor, my goals are:

1. To bring about a better understanding of the role and skills of the counselor

2. To improve guidance services for all students

3. To emphasize that guidance, if it is to be effective, must encompass the total school community.

IN SUMMARY:

The intent of this HANDBOOK is

To provide information that will lead

To MOTIVATING KIDS

TO THE MAX

(WITH YOUR HELP!)

In both the middle

And senior high school.

INTRODUCTION

E veryone who deals with young middle and high school students, whether as a parent or professional, does so for the betterment of these young people. In reality, it is a most demanding, tension filled and time consuming job. We do so because we believe in our students and want to help them fulfill their potential and lead happy lives. This message comes through every time we deal with our students. Our concern, kindness, and professionalism are a clear statement that we care for them. The satisfaction of our job comes from the good we can effect in the lives of our students. We must have faith that if our efforts seem to have no impact now, then in the years to come our advice will bear some fruit. Again, faith in our vision gives purpose to our work each day. This vision should be transferred to our students. They should be inspired to achieve. In whatever endeavor they choose, they, in their turn, should share their gifts for the betterment of humankind.

To be successful in delivering motivational guidance services, all aspects of the community must be included. Each member of the school community, at times, **fails** to cooperate in the venture and **you**, the reader, are asked to examine your role and performance.

Since the handbook is written from the perspective of the counselor, **you**, (the parent, the administrator, the teacher, the secretary or the intern), must make the transition to self-application. As you read each entry, no matter for whom the point is made, interpret it as it meets your particular needs and interest.

Occasionally, a reference is made to an acronym. For those who are unfamiliar with the acronym, there is a **Glossary of Acronyms** in the appendix of this handbook.

One of the major goals of the handbook is to give the school community a clear understanding of the role and function of the counselor. A clear understanding of the counselor's work will help to bring about mutual understanding and better school cooperation.

During the course of this handbook, an actual story or case study will be given to illustrate some theoretical point. It will be indicated with the title "**Anecdote**" or "**Case Study.**" Some anecdotes or case studies are descriptive, some heart warming, others far-fetched. Circumstances and genders may be changed, but all, nonetheless, are true. Though the anecdote is far-fetched, what is intended is to clarify a point. From it, a creative idea or sense of direction may be gained. Likewise, throughout the book are inspirational quotes to provoke further thought on the contents of the chapter.

In reading the handbook, there are times when information may seem repetitious.

This may be the case, but the circumstances surrounding the repetition will be different or coming from another prospective. In some cases, it is meant to be repetitious, since it is assumed that not everyone will read every chapter and the information is so important, it is worth repeating.

There are three central themes in the handbook:
1. **The need to give hope and direction to students**
2. **The need to establish good working relationships with staff**
3. **The need to approach guidance services as a total school effort**

Disclaimers

Not everyone will agree with the author's counseling style. Some of my ideas are controversial and may be contrary to other counseling practices. This is healthy since each counselor is unique. Take what is best out of the idea and use it. **Hitch hike on an idea and be creative in your own way.**

PART I

GUIDANCE
AND THE SCHOOL
COMMUNITY

CHAPTER 1

Guidance and Parents

Parents are their children's best advocates. The nature of this
book is to assist in that task. The more informed parents are, the
more productive will be their efforts.

Prize Education!

There is nothing more important than the interest parents take in
their son or daughter's education. Their involvement in academic
excellence, athletic activities, social events and family activities
contribute to the mindset of their children. Young people absorb their values
from their parents. The priority parents place on education is generally
reflected in their children's success in school. Nothing contributes more
to this success than a good working relationship between the parents and
the school staff. When there is frequent communication, there is sound
advice passed back and forth. **Education is not an overnight event; it
is a gradual and growing process and if parents and staff are in**

frequent contact along the way as partners, it produces growth. This concept applies to the unmotivated, the learning disabled, as well as the excelling student.

Cases Study

In the course of observing students in the hallway and later confirmed by a physical education teacher, a counselor observed a dramatic change in a student. The student began to associate with a new set of "friends." His grades began to slip, and his interest in team sports waned. Observation is one thing; action is another. Out of concern, the counselor took it upon herself to call the parents and share with them her observations about the perceived changes in their son's values, and choice of new friends. The parents were most grateful for this information and confirmed that they were seeing the same pattern at home. Together, the counselor and the parents began working on strategies to steer the boy in the right direction. In a sense, a partnership was formed at that moment. There was no need to inform the boy of this relationship; sometimes it is better for the counselor just to play his/her recognized role. Advice from someone other than the parent is generally more acceptable to teenagers, rather than advice that the student feels is coming from the parents through the counselor.

Good Parents—Bad Kids

Over the years, counselors are asked the question by good and caring parents when their children are in trouble, fail to do homework, are unmotivated and easily influenced by their peers, **"Where did we go wrong?"** And the answer counselors can only give is, **"Nowhere."** The counselor should alleviate the sense of guilt that good parents feel. There are forces in our society, values and mores, which are alien to the way that children should behave, and that parents have no influence over. Peer pressure, social trends, and character defects are not always within parents' ability to change. In dealing with such parents, counselors must re-enforce the belief that they are not at fault. Parents must keep on trying and not lose **hope** that through their good efforts a turn around will take place.

Overly Involved Parents

Some parents dominate their child's academic life. They are in on every quiz, assignment and grade the student receives. They do not do the work for the student nor do they enable the youngster. However, they direct and demand that the student complain about grades which are not high enough. They insist that parent conferences be held over the slightest issue, and they are constantly calling the counselor to get messages to the student or to intercede with a teacher. This is a difficult role for the counselor. Simply to tell the parent that what they are doing is wrong, will not work. They will ignore this advice and continue their demanding style. At the same time, the counselor has to work with the student to free him/her from unwarranted parental control. When some students become over-directed, they become passive aggressive, ignore the directives of the parent and begin to do poorly. A rational approach with the parent will help, but the help of a therapist may be necessary. Gradually, the parents should be led to see the error of their ways. At times, the counselor has to become the bridge that helps the parent to back off and give their son or daughter the confidence and freedom to handle their own affairs. Only in this way will students develop the necessary skills to function independently when they are on their own or ready to go off to college.

Overly Anxious Parents

Every year counselors will run into an overly anxious parent. Usually they are very unfamiliar with the school's polices in all areas: grades, transcripts, absentee procedures, etc. When these procedures are explained, they are again concerned that they are properly implemented for their youngster. This is a form of compulsive behavior. They have to check on everything. A firm understanding with the parent that the counselor will make sure that all areas are covered will help but will not make the problem go away. However, it will help to shorten conversations. Unfortunately, with this type of parent if they are not satisfied, he/she will not hesitate to get involved with the principal or superintendent. Visits to the school are frequent. If the counselor can come to an understanding that he/she can only give a short response because of a heavy caseload, time will be saved and the parent satisfied. An initial description of the counselor's heavy caseload will help the parent understand the need for brevity. (See Addendum 1.)

Overly Liberal Parents

Overly liberal parents work at odds with their school. Every school is a structured society in which students have to conform to basic rules. To allow young people to assume absolute responsibility for their actions is simplistic. We all have the right to fail, but parents do not have the right to walk away from the consequences. If continued lateness, incomplete homework, lack of study, cutting, truancy, etc., go unchecked, they jeopardize the student's chances for success. Failure not only breeds demoralization and negative self-concepts, but also sets the student entirely on the wrong course.

Case Studies

1. The father of a sixteen-year-old boy brought his son as a birthday present to a female strip joint in New York. At the same time, the father failed to monitor the son's poor academic performance. The parent's liberal attitude towards his son's education and moral values prevented him from providing the guidance and limits necessary for his son to succeed. Such behavior demonstrates a lack of values and foresight. In this instance, ironically, the young man pursued a similar "profession" as male go-go dancer while still in high school.

2. When a student is truant and the school phones to verify it, the parent should confirm it. If the parent does not and backs the student so that he/she will not get in trouble, it is enabling the student in the worst possible way.

In cases such as these:

1. The job of the school is to be in contact with the parent when the student fails to meet his/her school responsibilities.

2. The job of the parent is to work with school officials to bring about accountability.

3. The job of the counselor is to work with the student and parent to bring basic structure into the life of the student.

The PTA and Guidance Services

In many schools, counselors are leery of the PTA. This very strong organization wheels great influence with the principal and superintendent. It represents the parents of the community and receives much feedback from the community. Sometimes, the PTA may misunderstand the work of the counseling department. More open communication, to foster a clearer understanding of the work of the guidance department, is essential. A handbook of counseling services, such as this book, may shed some light on the role of the counselor, but a more effective approach is to make sure that at least one counselor is at all PTA meetings. After all, it is supposed to be a parent-teacher organization. Keeping the PTA up to date and informing it of coming events and programs are the ticket to communication. Just the fact that there is a representative from the guidance department, demonstrates interest. In addition, should any point come up regarding counselors or guidance programs, someone is there to clarify the issue. The idea that counselors need not attend, have tenure and cannot be touched by the PTA is nonsense. **PTA recommendations for new programs, different initiatives, and varied approaches, which do not have counselor input, may become counter-productive for the guidance department.** Parents acting in good faith who make recommendations for changes in the counselors' "modus operandi," may not comprehend all the ramifications. Consequently, frequent communication between the guidance department and the PTA will obviate these kinds of problems.

Case Study

A very vocal and demanding parent came unannounced and without an appointment to get some help in compiling college applications. This was at a very busy time of the year when college applications were due and schedule changes had to be made. The counselor had every right to send her away since she did not have an appointment. Instead, he found a way of helping the parent while also communicating how busy he was. Students were backlogged, waiting to see the counselor. The parent had all sixteen of her son's applications. The counselor told the parent he would direct her in competing her part of the applications while he saw, at the same time, some students in his office. He organized packets of non-confidential information for the parent to place in each application. The counselor also knew that none of the students he was about to see had personal problems and were there simply to request schedule changes. This was a good learning experience for this very vocal parent to see students serviced. The counselor proceeded to assist the waiting students while also directing the parent with her task, as needed. This approach took a skill obtained through years of experience in task management.

Four things were accomplished:
1. The parent received the necessary help with her task.
2. Students were seen and their needs met.
3. The parent came away with a greater appreciation and understanding of the work of the counselor.
4. The counselor now had an advocate in the community.

Who is Responsible?

There are two reasons generally why students are at home. They are suspended or are at home sick. Who on the school staff is responsible for getting them their homework assignments? Each school has to work out a policy. The main thing is that the policy is set down very clearly. If not, no one likes to assume extra work and the student may not be serviced.

Homework

There are times when parents request homework to be collected by the counselor for their temporarily sick child. Collecting homework can become a chore and an additional responsibility. If the counselor has e-mail, this is the best way to inform staff members that they should supply the necessary work and drop it off at the guidance office or e-mail it to the parent. It can be suggested to parents that the quickest way to get homework is to keep in touch with teachers directly by phone or e-mail. Also, suggest that their child's dependable friends can be the best conduit between teacher and student. However, it is achieved, **a follow up** with the parent that the homework is being delivered, helps to build good parent-counselor relationships. If the counselor initiates the request for homework, no matter how it is sent home, the final responsibility for the delivery of all the homework assignments is that of the counselor. Simply delegating the responsibility is not enough.

Reports

Parents, administrators or the Pupil Personnel Services Team usually request progress reports through the counselor. Progress reports provide an up-to-date assessment of the student. Teacher input may determine alternate plans or placement for the student. Counselors should advise teachers that when they receive weekly progress reports on a student, to complete and return the form as soon as possible. This is necessary so that the counselor will have the information for parental and guidance meetings. Inform the teachers that the delay in the return of reports may mean the difference in the decision making process. Detailed information on missing homework, disruptive behavior in class, etc. will determine corrective procedures. Should a teacher not return the report, a personal visit by the counselor explaining the purpose and possible outcomes will facilitate future requests. To report the teacher to an administrator for not delivering the report in a timely fashion does not bring about good relationships or future cooperation. Take the time and effort to speak with the teacher. This will bear more fruit in the long run.

Processing Progress Reports

Parents frequently request weekly progress reports to assess a student's progress. There are several ways to do this:

1. Send a packet of progress reports to the parents and have them issue them to the student every Thursday and have it returned on Friday afternoon. The student at the end of class asks each teacher to quickly rate a single progress report form with a section for each teacher. and the

counselor. The student is instructed that the counselor signs off at the end so that he/she can read and copy the document. Allow a two-day delivery in case some teachers are absent. Inform the parents that their son or daughter should be penalized if he/she does not comply.

2. If this method does not work, usually because the student does not barter to request the information or makes some excuse that the teacher was not available, the counselor should have the secretary issue individual reports directly to the teachers on Wednesday and request that they to be returned to the counselor on Thursday. Photocopy and file one copy and send the other home to the parent on Friday. The two-day turn around, again, is to allow for teacher absences, etc.

Honor Courses

When teachers deny students honors or AP courses, there should be an understanding on the part of the teachers that parents and counselors are notified. Counselors should stress to the teachers that their decisions need to be explained to parents, **by them**. Teachers have all the reasons for their recommendations. In addition, parents will ask questions about the nature and content of the course that teachers are more familiar. They can explain nuances that the counselor is unaware. Since no one likes to be the bearer of bad news, some teachers are very reluctant to call parents on these matters. If the counselor can be a facilitator in this thorny situation, both the parent and the teacher appreciate it. However, the teacher **must** be involved.

Long Range Relationships

In dealing with students, it is important to realize that many of the counselor's students have siblings and that the relationship he/she establishes with the first child will have an impact on all the children who follow. A good rapport and working relationship with the older student and parents will be passed along to younger siblings.

Out of District Students

There are circumstances, for the good of students, where they are taken out of their middle or high school and placed in an alternate school. If the home school offers a diploma to students placed out of district, the counselor should be sure to check that they have completed all graduation requirements and that a diploma is ordered for them. This is a key issue for these students and their parents. Their home school diploma represents an achievement in the course of a long struggle. Additionally, counselors should keep in contact with these students as a sign of their support and interest.

Home Schooling

If a parent wants to do home school schooling for their child, the request is usually made through the assistant superintendent and guidelines established.

Private Schooling for Special Education Students

Children, who attend private schools and are classified, are entitled to special education services from their home district. The counselor should reassure such parents that the home district is obliged under law to provide services. (For more information on services for Special Education children see **Chapter 6.**)

Absenteeism

If a student is underage and is adamant in refusing to attend school, a PIN'S (Pupil In Need of Supervision) should be filed. If the parents are at fault in this matter, the Child Protective Service (CPS) should be contacted. The counselor should not be concerned about disclosure since CPS does not reveal the source of the complaint.

Sharing the Burden

At times parents or students request lengthy and time-consuming information about various colleges or agencies. Involving parents and students in achieving the request serves to educate the parent or student and saves time for the counselor. This would include such items as:

1. Contacting colleges to send applications,
2. Checking on the status of an application,
3. Finding out about college requirements, etc.
4. Researching scholarship information
5. Finding out information on summer programs
6. Finding information on specialized programs for the gifted
7. Etc.

All of the above can be handled in the counselor's office if the parent or student is present. They can look up the phone number of the college or agency and make the call under the counselor's supervision. If applicable, the counselor can get on the phone and possibly advocate for the student. This is good public relations and an effective and productive way to teach students and parents how to obtain information and to be self-advocates. In addition, the internet is a helpful tool and supplies a source of information that parents and students should tap into whenever possible.

Don't Be Off-handed about It

There are two ways to handle parents or students who are over demanding in their requests for information. The first is to be off handed about it and simply refer them to a source. This approach gets the job done, but the parents see it as a lack of interest and another way for the counselor to avoid work. The second is to explain that as a counselor your job is to educate the student and the parent in the proper way to procure resources. Tell them the resource and ask them to report back to you so that together the results can be discussed. This is regarded as being constructive and concerned.

College and Parental Involvement

Parents are an integral part of the college process. Having their son or daughter call the admissions office for detailed information on admissions criteria, college majors, etc. as described above, is a good technique for several reasons:

1. Parents can get a realistic appraisal of the child's chances of getting into a specific college.
2. It demonstrates an interest in that specific college on the part of the family and student.
3. It establishes a contact person.

(See Chapters 18 and 19 for more college information.)

Parents Right to Know

In high school, parents have the right to call upon the school for student grades. In college, this right reverts to the college student and the college deals directly with the student. Parents will not be sent grade reports, attendance notifications, progress reports; professors will not be calling, etc. Even if the parent is paying the bill, the college will only deal with the student. Colleges regard the student as an adult and will only have contact with the student. Consequently, do not expect the same nurturing services that the high school provides. In fact, the more proactive your son or daughter becomes in high school, the easier and quicker their adjustment to total independence in college.

Looking Ahead

Considerable information on applying to college will be found in Chapter 18 for Ivy League candidates, middle of the road students and for weaker students, with a prevention dropout program for struggling college students. Additionally, for parents with children who have learning disabilities, there is a special college section in **Chapter 6.**

"It is a wise man who knows his own child."
Shakespeare (As researched by Kathleen Dooley)*

*Throughout this handbook are various inspirational quotes and sayings. A number of friends, colleagues, and scholars were asked to read specific chapters and recommend a quote. Their names are mentioned in gratitude for their contributions both now and in the past.

CHAPTER 2

Guidance and the Student

Unsung Heroes

E very aspect of this handbook deals with enriching and improving
the lives of students. Although every aspect of the counselor's
work revolves around students, it is amazing how little counselors
and teachers know about their students. This is not for want of interest
or concern. Usually, school personnel find out what is troubling a student
after a horrific event occurs in the student's life. There are cases of
extreme poverty, alcoholism, child abuse, peer pressure, incest, family
sickness, and personal problems that students have to deal with on a
daily basis. What astounds both teachers and counselors is how these
students manage to carry on, meeting their obligations and succeeding
while carrying such heavy burdens. Whenever possible, this information,

without betraying confidentiality, should be shared among teachers, counselors and administrators. At some point, these students may crack or begin to fall apart and what they need most is compassion rather than discipline. Shared information helps to prevent a wrong approach to these students.

Student Anxiety

There are students who are subject to anxiety attacks, some for no apparent reason. When it hits them and they cannot contain themselves, it is reassuring for them to know that they can come to the counselor's office whenever they are experiencing such an attack. It not need be the counselor's office. The school nurse, psychologist, or social worker are equally appropriate personnel. This approach is valid after the student reveals his/her problem and the parents are contacted to verify it. A discussion should also be held with the parent on receiving outside professional services. A troubled student is best served when his/her parents and the counselor work together as a team to help overcome the student's problem. The main thing is that the student knows that he/she has an escape valve and that the counselor understands and will clear any problems due to absence from a class with the teacher in question. These suffering students have to be **told** specifically how to handle an anxiety attack and given assurances that they are welcome in the counselor's office. (An invaluable resource is a comfortable room in the guidance office where the student can relax and be observed.)

Lower Socio-economic Students

Counselors should be extremely sensitive not to underestimate the potential of lower socio-economic students. It is easy when kids come to school unprepared, out of control or apathetic to write them off as potential dropouts, and concentrate on the "potentially" college bound students. "Triage" has no place in education! These "at risk" kids may be very unaware of the challenging world in which they will have to survive and live. Many may come from homes filled with problems, poverty, abuse, etc. The mere fact that they are in school is heroic.

**The primary goal of each counselor should be
to help each of these "at risk" students
graduate with a high school diploma.**

If students in today's society do not have the basic skills required to make a better life for themselves, all other considerations fall short. Counselors must have the knowledge, the drive, and the concern to discover the gifts and capabilities of these seemingly lost souls, and guide them to a respected place in our society. The counselor's greatest challenges often yield the most significant rewards. While guiding students "at risk" is arduous, frustrating, and disappointing, never give up. The guidance counselor is often their last **hope** to overcome their problems and lead normal and productive lives. Who else do they have in such a key position?

"I got my diploma and it's filled in with my name, ERNEST GREEN. *And I feel good about it."* Ernest Green, first Negro to graduate from Central High School, Ark., 1958 (As suggested by James Arthur)

Case Study

The importance of giving hope and encouragement to students cannot be stressed sufficiently. Some students carry such heavy psychological baggage that they turn to drugs for relief. A young man, who had a severe case of acne, would come to school each day shrouded in a hood, baseball cap beneath and his head, bowed. Besides his physical appearance, he was classified as learning disabled. His self-concept was at an all time low. He was non-communicative and isolated except for a few companions who happened to be into drugs. Gradually, the combination of his physical appearance and his personal problems turned him to drugs and eventually to addiction. Despite rehabilitation treatment, he overdosed multiple times. There were times when he seemed to be coming out of it and his physical appearance changed. He even came back to school to speak of his addiction to students. All conditions seemed ripe for a long-term recovery. Unfortunately, his predilection for drug usage to solve his personal problems overcame his good intentions and once again, he overdosed. This time there was no recovery; the life of a potentially very fine young man was wiped out.

MUCH WAS DONE FOR HIM BY CARING PEOPLE...TOO LATE!
HAD SOME FORM OF STRONG AND CARING INTERVENTION OCCURRED VERY EARLY ON,
HE MAY HAVE BEEN BETTER PREPARED TO DEAL WITH LIFE'S ISSUES.

*"It is **HOPE** which maintains mankind."* Sophocles
(As attributed to Harry O'Connell)

Gay and Lesbian Students

It is ironic that the next topic after the tragic story related above concerns gay and lesbians. There is much sadness associated with young people who have made the decision to change their life style, some of whom eventually end up killing themselves from the sense of alienation they feel. Counseling gay and lesbian students is a real political and moral challenge. These young people are not struggling so much with their identity as the effect their decision will have on their family and the society in which they live. Young gay and lesbian students come to their counselor genuinely worried and apprehensive about their parents' reaction. They are concerned that they will not be able to convince their parents of their very strong feelings. They fear family alienation. They also suffer because they cannot give their parents the grandchildren that so many desire.

There is no better service the counselor can give them than to understand their suffering. No matter what the personal beliefs of the counselor, these young people need someone to whom they can express their feelings and who is compassionate.

Anecdote

Acceptance

A good example of understanding and acceptance is that of a mother and father who at a conference on suicide told their story. First, they related how one of their daughter's gay friends committed suicide under the great pressures of alienation and rejection. They did not want this to happen to their daughter. In their heart of heart's they wanted a straight daughter and grandchildren. However, their love for their daughter superseded all else. They decided to accept their daughter and her partner with open arms. When their daughter's partner was introduced as a medical intern, the mother was delighted and to both lighten the moment and put the young lady at ease, responded, "We may not have our wish of grandchildren, but we can say with pride that we now have a physician in the family."

Student Accountability

In every school throughout America, there are outstanding students whose deportment is always an example to the rest of the student body and they are in the majority. These students meet their obligations, never get into trouble and some even conduct themselves in a way that benefits, even inspires their classmates. Often times, the only thing you read in the local paper are students who misbehave. Students who misbehave are the exception to the rule and it is from this perspective that student accountability will be addressed. There are multiple aspects to this topic. So that this handbook does not become a catalogue of failings, the section on Student Accountability focuses on a limited amount of in school student problems most effectively addressed by the counselor. Student accountability for academic performance is treated under **Chapter 13, titled "Motivation."**

Beating the System

In addition to acting as bastions of support and understanding for students, counselors must also be realistic and deal with students who attempt to use the counselor to beat the system.

Anecdotes

"Student Faux Pas"

1. There is the story of a senior girl, who in cutting an appointment with her counselor, called the counselor and claimed to be the mother. Speaking as her mother she began, "I'm calling on behalf of my daughter and would like to explain MY absence from your counseling session."

2. A classic case of cheating was uncovered by a counselor when proctoring an exam. The counselor saw two students exchanging test papers to fill in the right answers. It was a mutual swap, one helping the other out when "dumb"founded. When confronted by the counselor, they swore up and down, with the most shocked and innocent expressions on their faces, that they were not cheating. The only problem was that one student wrote in black ink and the other actually wrote in red, which meant that each of their papers were written in two colors, black and red and their test papers resembled two checkerboards.

Cutting Class

Whenever students come to the counselor without an appointment and claim they are free, their schedule should be checked to confirm that they are not cutting a class. If they get away with this, it also causes bad feelings with the subject teacher. Some students use the counselor as an excuse for getting out of class. Counselors who cover for these students will develop a reputation for being soft on students. If this is the case, teachers will be reluctant to cooperate in the future.

Exact Time

On an occasion, students will leave the counselor's office and take the entire period off. Then they will claim they have been with the counselor the entire time. Needless to say, when dealing with staff, counselors have to be very exact in student accountability. Teachers will ask for the specific time the student left. Once a student understands there is both communication and cooperation between their counselor and teachers, they will be far less tempted to abuse the system for their own gain.

Notebook Passes

Some schools, instead of using a pass system, use the back of a notebook with a listing for date, time, place, and signature. The student carries the notebook at all times and uses it when visiting the counselor, etc. This is paper free but can easily be forged. In addition, students can at times conveniently forget the notebook.

Working the System

If the guidance office keeps an attendance log, some students like to sign it and cut a class. The guidance secretary should control the log so that students have to request a "sign in" and "sign out." If the log is left on the counter, students will saunter in, sign it, and have a free period for themselves.

Verifying the Claim

Some students, in the hope of deceiving the guidance counselor, will come to the counselor's office and claim that the teacher has given permission for them to be there. Some clever students in order to skip a test will use the counselor for an excuse. These students should be sent back for a pass verifying their claim. Once word gets out that the counselor demands accountability, instances of the type described above will be curtailed.

Passes

Counselors should inform teachers that when a student visits the guidance office with a pass, the student should return with the same pass indicating the date and time the student left the counselor's office. The counselor should also sign it, and all signatures checked.

Punitive Measures

The best preventative measure to assure that students will not continue such practices is the referral of the student by the counselor to the Assistant Principal or Dean of Discipline for punitive measures.

A Counselor's Misconception

Some counselors feel that in referring a student for punitive measures they will damage their relationship with the student. When a student uses a counselor, he/she already has no respect for the counselor. The student will only respect the counselor for doing the right thing and will return for continued service. When the student returns, the counselor should reassure the student that past mistakes are forgotten, (not to be repeated), and the counselor will always be there to help the student.

Frequent Cutters

If a counselor has a student who frequently cuts classes and requests a study hall because he/she has enough courses for the year, a good strategy is to place the student in an elective course. The rationale for this is that students need credits toward graduation and, additionally, a good grade will build up the student's GPA. Students who regularly cut classes need frequent checks and giving them a study hall opens opportunities for more cutting.

A Student's Word

Never take a student's word that a teacher or parent has agreed to a change of schedule, or permission to leave the building, or permission to go on a trip, etc. Some students love to play the teacher against the counselor or *"visa versa"* by falsely attributing permission to leave the class to the other. Get it in writing and always double check with the people involved.

Case Study

Do Not Be Trapped.

Students are very clever. They will take it upon themselves to drop a course by not attending the class. They may even tell the teacher that they have the counselor's permission. After a while, they will come to the counselor and claim they had the teacher's permission to drop the course and besides it is now too late to receive the credit. The natural tendency for the counselor would be to regard the situation as a "fait accompli" and drop the student from the course and place the student in a study hall. This is a dangerous procedure, since the counselor will be held accountable for dropping the student without due written process. The teacher is at fault for not reporting the student for cutting. There are some students who teachers would rather not have in their class and are glad to take a passive role by looking the other way and not reporting the student. They too have to be held accountable.

Absent or Truant

Never rely on the word of a student requesting a letter from the counselor to verify an absence. The following steps should be taken:

1. Verify the absence with the attendance office.
2. Touch base with the parent. There have been cases where the student claims to have been legitimately absent when in reality the student was truant. If the counselor takes the student's word, the counselor is blamed for not doing his job and for lack of judgment.

"This above all,
To thine own self be true
And it must follow as the night the day,
Thou canst not be false to any man." Shakespeare
(In tribute to Judge Peter A. Quinn)

CHAPTER 3

Guidance and the Counselor

The Damocles Sword

Few people realize the amount of accountability to which the counselor is subject. Some counselors are responsible for every aspect of their students' school performance including: scheduling, academic planning, school related social problems, out of district placement, academic failures, college planning, special education input, parental follow up procedures, clerical chores, record keeping, SAT information, career planning, etc. If the counselor makes a mistake in any one of these areas, the counselor is called to task, sometimes quite severely. No wonder the counselor is under pressure a great deal of the time just to make no mistakes! When you factor in writing reports and college recommendations, and meeting deadlines, still more pressures are added. Sadly, all too many of the counselor's chores are clerically related, and take away a significant amount of time from actual counseling.

Understanding the Special Skills Needed to Be Counselor

To understand the role of the counselor, it is necessary to understand the special skills and talents needed to get the job done including:

1. The talent required to motivate and counsel students
2. The organizational skills to deal with multiple tasks
3. The ability to handle pressure.
4. The expertise to advise seniors on colleges
5. The psychological skills to deal with all kinds of problems, from social adjustment to suicide ideation, from poor self-concepts to poor motivation, etc.
6. The capacity to relate to fellow staff members
7. The capacity to work hard
8. The experience and knowledge to deal with a range of topics **(Addendum 1.)**
9. **The gift of a nurturing personality**
10. The capacity to walk the tight rope that brings all members of the school community together
11. The ability to deal with their public in a way that is productive and not adversarial
12. The expertise in using modern technology.
13. Etc.

Continuity of Services

One may ask, "Why in this handbook for middle and high school guidance services are there so many references to such a wide range of topics?" The answer is relatively simple. Guidance services are multi-faceted; guidance is a continuum of many services and the earlier students and parents begin to understand what guidance services offer, the greater the educational development and benefits to students. Consequently, a middle school student who understands the need for good study habits to achieve a superior final GPA in high school is more likely to be motivated and focused. When parents understand the academic demands of the SAT exams, the more guided they are helping in the long-range preparation of their child. The more the counselor engages middle school students to express their feeling, the more open they will be in high school. They will feel more comfortable in expressing their concerns when they may be under pressure. The more middle school teachers are cognizant of the requirements of AP or IB courses, the more they are guided in their instruction. Teachers should not teach for exams, but knowledge of these exams gives a sense of direction. The more administrators understand the flow and timing of guidance services, the more understanding they will be in their requests for lengthy reports. **The long-range contribution of effective guidance services from the earliest years in academic, career planning and college placement cannot be underestimated, resulting in far more desirable outcomes.**

The Psychological Difference

Some middle school students, advancing from the elementary school, experience a real transition problem. Moving from contained classes in earlier grades, where they have worked out their position in this small society to a much larger and diverse society in the middle and senior high school, poses distinct challenges for some. Instead of relating to one teacher and twenty odd students, they are now required to adjust to four or five teachers and make relationships with ninety or more students. Some of these students experience social problems, from non-acceptance to being bullied, from being inhibited to acting out, etc. Besides the normal chores of the counselor, greater emphasis has to be placed on group counseling and developing social skills in the middle school. For information on forming coherent and lasting group counseling sessions that deal with these problems, **see Chapter 16, subtitle "How to Form a Group-Counseling Program."**

"Connect Four"

A fine example of the difference between the psychological approaches in the middle and high school counselor is the technique surrounding games and sports used to break down barriers of inhibition and shyness. In the middle school, the counselor may use a game such as "Connect Four" to put the student at ease and help the student acclimate to the counselor who is trying to get him/her to open up and talk. The high school counselor would regard this approach as not appropriate for an upper class person. However, to breakdown the barriers of inhibition and shyness on the high school level, the counselor may try to use icebreakers by referring to a sport or other special interest. Each counselor must assess the approach that will best bring the student out of his/her shell. (So the next time the reader passes a middle school counseling office and observes the counselor playing a game with a student, do not rush to report him/her to the "gaming commission" for wasting time on the job.)

A Massive Undertaking

Throughout this handbook are multiple suggestions for proactive counseling. A counselor reading it could easily wonder, "When am I going to get the time to put into practice all these suggestions?' The answer is that **not** all suggestions have to be implemented. A gradual attempt to implement some would be a good start. When they are spread out over the course of the year, the task is more feasible. The secret is, if the suggestion appeals to you, work it into your daily dealings with students. Try to discard old practices that consume time, and work in the new procedures that benefit students. Then, not all the suggestions will seem such a massive undertaking and will become manageable.

Anticipate Problems

Counselors should try to anticipate possible problems of a serious nature (i.e. violence, suicide, bulimia, etc) and bring them to the attention of the C.S.T (Child Study Team) or the appropriate school committee. Identifying a problem **early** gives the counselor the advantage of obtaining advice and implementing a solution that is in the best interest of the student.

In the Field

The counselor should make it a practice to leave his/her desk at least once a day and circulate throughout the building. It is amazing how much contact the counselor will have with students and the amount of work that will be done. This practice is such an asset to the counselors that it needs to be developed as a habit. (**Addendum 2**) Some counselors, initially, may seem awkward standing in the hallway. In time, students and teachers will look for the counselor in the accustomed spot. And, surprisingly, they will miss you when you are not there.

Case Study

At the beginning of the day, by standing in a central area (main corridor, entrance to the building, outside the guidance office, etc.), the counselor picks up a great deal of information about his/her students that cannot be obtained by sitting at one's desk. The practice allows the counselor to get a "visual." It may be for only fifteen minutes, but much can be accomplished, far more than remaining behind a closed door and waiting for students to seek you out.

Advantages:

1. Students who look undernourished, or appear to be losing weight (possible bulimia) or appear to be gaining a great deal of weight can be spotted by the alert counselor.

2. Students who have recently broken an arm or leg can be identified and may need someone to carry their books, take notes, or run interference in the hallway, etc.

3. Students who are visually upset (crying, angry, depressed, etc.) can be spotted and helped.

4. Cliques, isolates, bullies, homework copiers, etc. can be identified.

5. Students developing relationships or broken relationships become apparent. Even a boy and girl friend coming to school both freshly showered and their hair still wet, are all obvious indicators to the trained counselor.

In addition to gathering information, the counselor has a chance:

1. To greet his/her students
2. To be available to answer quick questions
3. To pick off students whom the counselor wants to remind about testing, follow up chores, etc.

A great deal of public relations work can also be accomplished at this time:

1. Teacher contacts can be made and, by so doing, the counselor is regarded as accessible. It is also a chance to socialize with teachers and build counselor-staff relations. (Important and critical to effective counseling!)

2. The counselor's presence in the hallway aids in keeping discipline which is also greatly appreciated by administrators. Counselors are not expected to do supervision but the mere presence of the counselor is preventative.

3. The counselor's presence in the hallway conveys the notion that the counselor is not always bound to a desk but out among his/her students.

4. Often times, parents pass by and it is a chance to say hello or deal with a student problem. The public becomes aware that the counselor is attempting to reach out to students.

Resist the Temptation

You may say, "It is all well and good for someone not carrying my caseload to be advocating for more time in the hallways when I have a whole bunch of emails to read and answer or college recommendations to write before the first period bell rings." This is a valid excuse, but one that puts clerical work before a personalized relationship with students. You choose.

Know Yourself

There are times, under the pressure of the job, when dealing with parents who are completely out of order, that the counselor has to refrain from telling them off, even politely. The counselor must recognize his/her breaking point and hold back. Calm down, resist the temptation to unload. Remain a professional with them, at all times. This will save the counselor many problems. It is more important to have parents on your side rather than against you as an enemy, badmouthing you in the community for years until their son/daughter graduates. It is all about the way the counselor handles the situation.

Caution

At times students may come to the counselor's office exhilarated by success (i.e. acceptance into college or winning a middle school award, which the counselor helped the student to achieve, etc.) and they wish to give the counselor a hug or kiss on the cheek. Settle for a happy face instead and always keep the door to the office open. Be friendly but not overly familiar. If the counselor must receive a hug, step outside the office, where the secretaries are witnesses.

Anecdote

In the whacky world we live, it is conceivable that a counselor may make enemies. On one inauspicious occasion, a note to the principal accused a counselor of molesting a girl in his office. The note was not signed, and therefore given no credence. It was also to the counselor's advantage that he always kept his door open when seeing students. The door can remain open and yet be private if the counselor situates students so that the counselor can be seen but the student is not visible from the outside.

Tenure and Arrogant Parents

Because a counselor may have tenure, it does not give him/her the leeway to be impertinent. The guiding principle should be, "What is best for my students is how I approach things." Turn your relationship with an arrogant parent into a positive and appreciative one. Give them time and educate them to your role. It is far better to have a happy ally than a vindictive parent.

Check It Out

When confronted with a difficult situation from an administrator, etc. and the counselor does not have an immediate answer, is stymied or has no reply at all and needs time to come up with an intelligent answer, simply indicate that you will check your notes and get back to him or her. This will give the counselor time to think out the problem and obtain advice.

Confer with Your Department Head

When in doubt in a difficult situation, the counselor should always confer with her/his department head. Department heads are in that position because of their training and experience and are available to share their expertise as needed. If the counselor does not have a good working relationship with the department head, seek out someone on the faculty who is trusted and obtain advice. Never try to solve all your problems by yourself.

First Contacts

When greeting new students who are seeing the counselor for the first time, make sure you put them at ease. They do not know what to expect. This first meeting is so important to set the tone of your relationship and to develop positive feelings. Encourage them to return in a few days just to say hello and to let you know how they are doing. Tell them to be sure to say hello in the hallways and, in spite of the fact that they are new, the counselor cares for them and wants to help them succeed.

Positive Advice

Whenever the counselor is dealing with a negative situation such as failing grades, poor conduct, failure to do homework etc., it is always best to be straightforward. However, it is advisable always to end up with some form of encouragement, a strategy, and a positive sense of direction. It is the counselor's job to move forward and to give students **a sense of hope**. How many are the horror stories told by students of their counselor years later? They will refer to him /her, as "the worst counselor in the world!"

He said, "I never could get into college."

She said, "I should drop out of high school."

He said, "I was aiming too high with my career ambitions."

She said, "I would never amount to anything."

*"To give **hope***
Is to give the ability to cope." Unknown
(As attributed to Sheila Manning)

Know the Parameters of Your Job

It is important that all new counselors know the parameters of their job. It is wise never to take on the work of a teacher or other school personnel. If a student is failing a subject and a teacher directs the counselor to call the parents, the counselor's response should be that since he/she does not have all the information on the student, it is best to have the teacher make the **first** call with specific information. If there is a need for a follow up call, the counselor can then offer to make it. In the mean time, the counselor should send for the student.

Professional Compassion

There are times when counselors must use all their skills to guide students through difficult times. It may mean an extra effort and creativity to achieve this goal, especially when many people are involved and the circumstance is extraordinary.

Case Study

A case in point involved a young man who was on Homebound Instruction because of a nervous break down. The student could not do all the assignments that were sent home. He failed to get a passing grade because of his mental condition at the time. The counselor made an extra effort to visit all of the student's teachers and explained the circumstance in detail. Together they worked out a time line and assignments that realistically could be achieved by the student. This approach was far more conducive to the student's mental condition. By tailoring the assignments to meet the student's needs (yet maintaining the integrity of the courses) the student succeeded. In the counselor's busy world, the homebound student could easily have been overlooked and the student would have been set back a year.

Effective Communication System

Each school has its methods for sending for students to come to the guidance office. On those occasions when the system does not work, the counselor should "rise up" and make the contact him/herself. Walking the hallways, the counselor will have the opportunity to communicate with other students as well. In addition, you will be a visible presence to teachers.

Taking Students Out of a Class Room

Before the counselor **personally** takes a student out of a class for counseling purposes, be sure to have an arrangement with the teacher to do so. Some teachers are very touchy about this. Once an understanding is reached, follow the procedures agreed upon (except in an emergency). Regarding the student taken out of the classroom, be sensitive to the student in the manner in which this is done. This is especially so if the student does not know why. As soon as the counselor gets the student in the hallway, put the student at ease. Usually the student thinks he/she is in trouble, especially the younger ones who do not know the counselor well.

It is also wise for the counselor to make it a practice to avoid taking a student out of a course that needs consistency of attendance such as math, foreign language, science, etc.

Case Study

If the counselor has a good relationship with the teacher from whose class a student must be taken, a technique to put the student at ease is first to chat briefly with other students in the room. Students enjoy someone who comes into the classroom and chitchats with them. Then, quietly sidle up to the student in question and ask him/her to step outside. Once outside, immediately put the student at ease. This method is better than simply asking the student to step outside. This places too much attention on the student.

Additionally, some teachers are so gregarious that they will encourage the students in welcoming the counselor, often bantering with the counselor. If so, this sets up an even more casual atmosphere in which to deal with students. On one occasion, the counselor was having such a good time, he became so distracted that when he turned to leave the classroom, he opened the door to the closet and walked in, giving the students a good laugh. That one mishap and friendly bantering endeared him to the students.

Make Special Note

In sending for students by a note, if there is a special reason why the student **must be seen**, please indicate it. Regrettably, some teachers ignore the normal request because of the serious nature of what is going on in class. Every effort should be made to help teachers realize that a simple request from the counselor may have multiple ramifications. The same holds true for progress reports on students.

Case Study

When a student is being evaluated by the CSE (Committee on Special Education), public knowledge is not made of this. Should a progress report be sent to a teacher, usually there is no indication of the reason. Some teachers are lax about returning them. Yet, the reports of the teachers and the information they provide are essential to the outcome of the meeting. If a student is to be placed out of the building because he/she is disruptive and a threat to other students, this must be documented. When there is no supporting evidence for this, an injustice is done to both the committee and the student. If, for example, a student is physically abusive to other students and especially to girls and the teacher fails to document it, the committee is the unable to act without the facts.

Don't Fail to Verbalize Your Concern for Your Students

All counselors pride themselves on the concern, love, and interest they have for their students. It is a message that counselors are always trying to communicate to their students. However, this is not always the case. At times, it needs to be verbalized in one form or another. There is nothing wrong in saying to students that you really want to help them because they are important and you care for them. Counselors can say it by their tone of voice, by the expression on their face, by the way they follow up on the student's behalf. If counselors come across as perfunctory, no matter how much work they do for students, it is regarded as part of the job, and not as a genuine concern for their well-being.

"My Counselor Is Never Available"

A common complaint of students is that, "My counselor is never available." At times, this is true because the counselor is so busy with transitional planning, college planning, scheduling, CSE meeting, etc. When the counselor has students piled up outside his/her office and cannot see them, it is a good practice to call all of them in for a brief meeting, explaining why he/she is so busy. Then ask the nature of each student's visit so the counselor can plan when to see the student. Often times a quick answer will suffice to direct some of the students. In matters of a personal nature, a follow-up is necessary. The message will come across, though busy, the counselor is responsive and a reputation for unavailability will diminish.

"The Two Faces of Eve"

At times, when a student comes to see the counselor, he/she may be wearing a mask. The face that is worn is that of a student in need, who is misunderstood, and innocent of any wrongdoing. In reality, it may be that the student is there because he/she may not be getting along with a specific teacher. The face the teacher sees is that of a student who is not doing his/her homework, is disruptive in class, and does not respond to encouragement. The student may regard this as harassment and the teacher as an issue of accountability. The job of the counselor is to uncover the true face by speaking with the teacher. Experience is a great asset.

A knowledge of the teacher's classroom style and of the student's past history will help dictate the right approach.

Emergencies

When the counselor comes across a problem that has developed into an emergency (such as suicides ideation, depression, severe anger, a violent intent, etc.), he/she should immediately refer the situation to the school psychologist and an administrator should be informed. (Follow school policy on these matters.) Also, develop the skill of anticipating possible problems and referring them to the child study team for consideration. Anticipating problems makes the counselor proactive and establishes a reputation for being both incisive and involved.

Students Who May Not Graduate

There are instances when eighth graders or seniors may not graduate because of possible academic failures. The counselor should anticipate this possibility and have on file letters, conferences, etc. that have taken place. Counselors never want to be in the position of not having warned the parent. Although it is the student who fails, it is human nature to blame someone else.

It is likewise the duty of the teacher to notify the parent beyond the report card. If the teacher asks the counselor to do so, it should be explained to the teacher that for the sake of both the student and the teacher, personal contact has to be made. In most schools, this is policy.

Whenever the counselor does follow up on this matter, it is advisable to send a photocopy of the communication to the teacher and department head. In most schools, the same approach holds true for underclassmen that give indications of failing a course for the year.

Alternate Ways to Meet Graduation Requirements

In New York State, Regent exams are a graduation requirement. In the matter of Regents, there are alternative ways to meet these requirements. New York State allows for designated results from the SAT I and SAT II exams to meet Regent's requirements. Each state has its alternate procedures. They should be investigated.

Homebound Students

When students are on homebound instruction for health reasons, the counselor, or more appropriately the nurse, should verify that they are non-contagious for the protection of the homebound teachers.

Meetings

Whenever the counselor has a team/parent/teacher conference regarding a specific student, the counselor should bring the student's schedule, transcript, copy of records and all other data pertaining to the student's past and present performance. If the counselor has time, send out progress reports before the meeting. Nothing enhances a counselor's reputation more than being well prepared for a parent conference.

Use of E-mail

A wonderful way to contact teachers and notify them of parental concerns, as well as a way to help individual students, is through e-mail. Regarding the e-mails sent by the counselor, he/she should save a paper copy and place it in the student's file to verify that the counselor has acted on the issue involved.

Notifying Teachers

Whenever a student is seriously sick, or there is a special circumstance at home, or a problem arises that the counselor can share with the student's teachers, it is well to do so. It is good public relations, helps the teachers understand and benefits the student.

Counselor as "Mover"

An aspect of the counselor's role, beyond counseling or clerical academic chores, is to be an advocate for change. Much of the good counselors do is achieved by collaborating with others.

1. If a counselor has an arrangement with a parent to observe a student's friends, especially if they are having a poor influence on the student, the counselor can report to the parents so they can take action.

2. At a PPS meeting, if the counselor recommends a change of school for the good of the student, based on solid information, the school psychologist or director of special education must act to implement a plan. Likewise, if the student can be served better by some one of the same sex, the referral should be made.

3. In the case of a student whom the counselor knows needs to be disciplined for cutting or misconduct, he/she must act. If the counselor's advice to the student does not effect a change, the counselor should share discretely the information with the dean of discipline. This is especially so if the counselor's disclosure is not of a confidential nature and will not violate a trust. For example, if a counselor sees a student smoking on school grounds, he/she should report the student. The student will be helped and the counselor's role will be preserved. Much of the good counselors do is achieved by having others share in bring about the necessary changes.

Counselor as "Leader"

A major role of the counselor is to assess school programs, policies, and procedures that affect students. Administrators, who at times do not see the outcome of their decisions as they affect students in the long run, make changes. It is the counselor's role to bring the negative aspects of such changes to their attention. If, for example, there is no provision in the master schedule for required courses to be placed in the morning for students who attend special programs in the afternoon, the administrator in charge of the master schedule should be notified, etc.

In some circumstances, whole programs that assist students have to be defended. Many administrative decisions are motivated by financial concerns. If the good of the students is at stake, **the counselor must bring the negative effects of these changes to the attention of administrators** so that they are better able to evaluate their decision and perhaps find another way to economize.

Students and Drugs

If a counselor has been informed that a student is doing serious drugs and counsels the student to no effect, he/she has an obligation to follow up to protect the well being and safety of the student. To retain a good relationship with this student, seek the aid of the drug coordinator or school nurse immediately and work out a plan. It is also recommended that the counselor refer his/her concern to the Pupil Personnel Team for consideration. The student's name need not be mentioned, but advice sought.

Students who claim to be drug-free but still have their teachers coming to the counselor indicating their concern, must be double-checked. One of the characteristics of drug involvement is the constant assertion by the individual that he/she is **drug free**. Parents should not be so naïve as to take their child's word. Sustained drug testing is the best verification.

Never Give Anything Away without Getting Something in Return

In the course of advocating for students, counselors go to great lengths. Schedules are changed; teachers brought into the loop; special arrangements made. Most students are very grateful for these services. However, it is at these times of gratitude that the counselor should encourage some beneficial promise or service from the student. It could be a promise for improved academic performance, a request to help a fellow student, or an invitation to do some volunteer work. (This advice applies to parents and teachers as well when they perform a service for a student.)

Anecdote

Counselors spend hours writing college recommendations. Some counselors choose not to read them to their students. Others do, but fail to mention the hours of work that went into producing a well-written recommendation. Regrettably, when some of theses students are accepted into college, they fail even to notify (let alone thank) their counselor who put so much work into their recommendation and application. As they say, "Eaten bread is soon forgotten." Hence, the necessity of educating young people not to take everything or anybody for granted.

Training Students to Be Accountable

During the course of counselor's work there are many times when parents, teachers, and counselors enable students by doing the greater part of their work: science projects, college essays, college applications, phone calls, e-mails, etc. As a result of this enabling process, students are not properly prepared to meet the challenges of college: registering, meeting deadlines, advocating for help, etc. The role of the counselor is to point out this deficiency and direct students how to become more self-reliant.

Anecdote

On one occasion, a student brought a large packet of college information to his counselor, requesting help. Upon reviewing the contents, the counselor was disappointed to see all that was required was the addition of a postage stamp. It was obvious to the counselor that the student did not even read the document, expecting the counselor to do all the work. From that point on, the student was encouraged and guided to be more self-reliant.

Additional Courses

Students who attend occupational training programs (BOCES) may receive credit for a course that is inherent in the career program, for example, math, and science in an auto technology course. Make sure, that if this is the case, these courses are listed in the student's record and, if appropriate, on the main transcript.

Be Proactive

There are many occasions in the course of the counselor's work when information (for example: summer school grades, AP scores, etc.) is not placed in the computer, or on official transcripts, etc. It is easy to clear up the counselor's part by notifying the guidance secretary. However, the counselor should also act to make sure that an error that affects all students is corrected across the board.

Departing Counselors

As counselors move on to other schools or retire, part of their legacy is to leave behind for the incoming counselor a master list of their students. This list should include a brief one or two word description of each student's major attribute or difficulty. Simple words like anxious, highly intelligent, failing, enabled, superior athlete, frequent cutter, generous volunteer, difficult parent, demanding student, etc., will help the new counselor to connect quickly with each student. This can be greatly simplified by putting a code number for each attribute or difficulty at the top of the page and placing a number along side the name of the student. The knowledge the departing counselor has gained over the years on each student can be passed on. Theses students, then, will be given the services they deserve. Elementary school teachers and middle school teachers may utilize this technique as their children move on from one school to the next.

Share the Wealth

Periodically, counselors discover information, new techniques, or creative ideas that will make the counselor look good in his work. While the tendency may be to keep this information to oneself, exemplary counseling involves a team approach and all information should be shared. In sharing, the counselor will have the benefit of receiving, in turn, the findings of his/her peers and at the same gain a reputation as a team player.

Professionalism

Every counselor is expected to keep up with the times, adjust to change and remain current in the field. Counselors may be written up if they fail to know the content of their field. This applies to college information, recent laws, new state education regulations, computer knowledge and anything that can help them better serve students.

Criteria for the Evaluation of Pupil Personnel Services Staff

Counselors who are concerned about evaluation and supervision may find useful information in **Addendum 8**, "Criteria for the Evaluation of Pupil Personnel Services Staff" and in the **Epilogue**. They contain an overview of the main responsibilities of a counselor and may form the basis for a counselor evaluation. Better to know what is expected than being blind-sided.

Counselor Failings

Throughout this handbook are negative references to all members of the school community including:

1. Parents who are "completely wrong" on school issues or are very lax with their children
2. Administrators who sweep their mistakes under the rug
3. Teachers who are sarcastic to their students
4. Secretaries who overstep their boundaries

5. Students who work the system and fail to meet their responsibilities

Every effort is made in this handbook to place the counselor in the best light. However, it would be unfair to criticize the school community without including some of the failings of counselors. What applies to **the counselor** may also apply to the school social worker, the school psychologist, administrators, department heads, secretaries, and anyone in a private office with a telephone. In all fairness to the above professional personnel, there are days and weeks on end when they are so harried they have no free time for personal concerns, nor are there free periods built into their schedules. Teachers have free periods built into their contract and are generally not accused of the following abuses. What is stated here are practices, which are wrong when exercised **in the extreme** and consume excessive professional time that should be spent with students:

1. Extended and unnecessary personal phone calls
2. Planning family events, weddings, reunions, etc.
3. A daily ritual of reading the paper, especially the sports section
4. Polishing fingernails
5. Paying bills
6. Duplicating personal documents
7. Making personal appointments
8. Use of the internet for personal matters: purchasing, planning trips, e-mails
9. Extended lunches
10. Spending too much time chatting with peers or secretaries
11. Closing the door and napping.
12. Etc.

As the old saying goes, "If the shoe fits….. it doesn't suit you… change it."

(Human nature being what it is, the author must also fess up to some of the above abuses….
Mea Culpa.)

Your zeal for the pupils under your guidance would be imperfect if you only expressed it in words. It will become perfect only if you practice what you are teaching them." John B. De La Salle

(As quoted in the writings of Louis Rush, FSC)

CHAPTER 4

Guidance and Administrators

It's Lonely at the Top

Few people fully understand the myriad and complex challenges facing the high school and middle school principal. Their areas of responsibility are virtually limitless, ranging from academic excellence to school safety, from school spirit to parental concerns, and all else in between. At times, the principal's priority, based on confidential information, may conflict with a counselor's advice. It is equally important for the counselor to understand the principal's role in decision making, as it is for the principal to understand the inner workings of guidance. Clarifying the principal's role is not the purveyance of this handbook. However, the object of this handbook is to provide principals with as much insight as possible into the nature of guidance. (Administrators are invited to review **The Epilogue and Addendum 10** for approaches to evaluating and improving guidance services for students.)

Case Study

Principals rise to their position though merit and service. Distinguishing themselves, they rise first as teachers then as assistant principals and finally as principals. In the normal course of this passage, an insight is gained into the role of the guidance counselor. However, even a close working relationship with counselors does not reveal every aspect of their work. There are times when economic cutbacks sometimes force administrators to place others in leadership roles for which they have no real training. Such is the case of many directors of pupil personnel services. The administrator will be certified in special education and school administration, but are asked to oversee the guidance department, nurse, psychologists, etc. With no real understanding of the intricacies of the counselor's role, these administrators will make requests that are neither timely nor in keeping with the overall guidance pattern. Optimally, a period of orientation and exchange should take place over an extended period of time to bring about a mutual understanding of each other's role.

An Alliance

The relationship between the guidance department and administration should be symbiotic. There is no way to measure how much administration depends on guidance for the well functioning of the school. The advice counselors give their principal is crucial to good outcomes. Counselors are a principal's liaison with the public; counselors are the principal's ear to the ground; counselors are the administrators' vehicle for the implementation of policy. Guidance is not only the nuts and bolts that keep the machine running but also the grease that keeps it humming. Guidance gives additional soul to the school by treating the human as well as the academic. On the other hand, guidance without the support of the principal is less effective. If the principal cares about the counselor's caseload, is supportive in difficult situations, promotes guidance programs and initiatives, and is not involved in an adversarial relationship, guidance is bound to be more effective.

Administrative Follow Up

When an administrator or principal gives the counselor an assignment, it is important that the counselor regards getting back to him/her with the results as a top priority. This applies as well when following up an inquiry from a parent. Expediting requests is the mark of an effective counselor and establishes his/her reputation as a competent and concerned counselor.

Don't Pile On

There are rare occasions at meetings when an administrator comes under the gun. The pent up feelings of faculty on certain issues are let loose and the principal is barraged with criticism and complaints. The counselor can decide to be part of the pile on or to ease off. Remember that the counselor still has to have a working relationship with the administrator and how the counselor handles this situation will effect future relations.

A Major Contribution

A very difficult situation, especially when parents are involved, is that teachers fail to deliver grades on time. If parents want information, it is embarrassing for the counselor not to have it. This is especially so at the end of the year when teachers fail to hand in their grades on time and leave for the summer. The counselors have to call parents to set up summer school for failing students. If the counselor calls a few days late for summer school registration because of untimely delivery of grades, parents will question the counselor's effectiveness and take him/her to task for the delay. "Will their child be able to register for summer school at this late notification? If not, what do we do?" Can you blame parents for being so upset? The teacher should answer these questions and not the counselor. A major contribution of the administration is to have a strong hand in avoiding these kinds of problems.

RICHARD O'CONNELL, ED. D.

Alert the Principal

Counselors have access to information from students that influences the running of the school and student safety. When students reveal to the counselor that a fight might take place or a student has a weapon in school or there is plan underway to bring violence into the building, the counselor **must** act on such knowledge since it concerns the health and safety of students. The counselor should get as much information as possible from the student before conferring with the principal on how best to proceed. In these cases, there is usually a procedure and a team to deal effectively with the problem.

Share Good News with the Principal

During the course of the school year, a student will achieve something of significance but will not be recognized. It may not be connected to a school club or organization, which has award ceremonies. In that case, an arrangement should be worked out with the principal to bring the student to the principal's office for a few words of recognition. This keeps the principal in touch with students. For the counselor, it is an opportunity to share with the principal some of the good work taking place in his or her school. (Note here the constant reference to the principal and the need for teamwork so frequently stressed throughout the handbook.)

Anecdote

How many are the children that go through high school, who are quiet and unassuming, and yet achieve on a high level? A very fine example was the work of three sisters who formed a classical music group and performed in long evening gowns for various charities, hospitals, and dignitaries from the United States and foreign countries. (**Cover**) By night, they were three beautiful Cinderellas and by day, normal teenagers wearing jeans and going about their school duties, undistinguishable from the rest of the student body. How many are there that achieve something of note in their outside activities and bring merit to the school but are not recognized? The simple act of the counselor, gathering such students and bringing them to the principal's office for a brief moment of recognition has a beneficial effect.

Share Problems

Counselors do not always have answers to every problem that arises. Sharing the problem with a department head or the principal will provide the counselor with added insights. Should things go wrong, the counselor is covered by his/her willingness to seek help.

Case Study

There are times when students reveal to the counselor some very strange information, which can pose a real dilemma. There was the incident where one of a student's friends, who happened not to be in the high school, was considering suicide. **Clearly, even though the student was outside of the school, action had to be taken.** The counselor should be sure to get as much information from the student as possible. Next, confer with the department head or the principal on how best to proceed, since this is a unique situation. Whatever the directive, a life could be at stake. (The same holds true for any student in the building who is at risk of suicide. In this case, there is usually a procedure and a team to deal properly with the problem.) For unique cases, follow the advice of the administrator. Simply to say that it is a matter outside the school and not the counselor's responsibility is a failure to act.

A Plea for Space

Many schools in the past were built with the concept in mind that counselors work one-on-one with students and therefore require minimal space. However, today's approach to guidance services now includes group counseling as well. Special education students have mandated counseling services included in their Individual Education Plans, which may be done in groups and performed by the guidance counselor. Middle school counselors respond to the many social adjustment needs of their students and utilize group-counseling sessions. **What is needed is more space so that students can have room for their chairs or to spread out on the floor and talk freely.** In the middle and senior high school, so much could be accomplished in small groups: counseling sessions, small group instruction, meetings with college representatives, filling out forms, etc., if only more space in the counseling office could be provided. (In the Epilogue, administrators are asked to contribute to guidance services as sign of their continuing interest. A group counseling/conference room would be a great addition.)

Spot It Early

There are two methods used by administrators, department heads, and teachers to avoid involvement or making a decision. They include either the, "Yes them to death method" or the "Ignore them to death method." The first is to say "yes" to everything the counselor requests and then do nothing about it. The second is to take the counselor's request under advisement and do nothing about it. These methods generally work because so much time goes by and the issue fades, but not in favor of the counselor or the student. The only approach for the counselor, once the technique is spotted, is to go "vis-à-vis" with the administrator or teacher with the objective of an immediate or direct honest answer.

Difficult Parents

Counselors occasionally deal with parents who are very difficult and demanding. If these parents do not get what they want, they go directly to the principal or department head. In addition, if they are not satisfied there, they will go to the superintendent. Before this happens, the principal or department head should be alerted that they are on their way. The principal should be filled in with background information, the steps the counselor has taken and why the parents will be "difficult."

A Different Point of View

Principals and department heads are not omniscient and will occasionally see things from a different point of view. It is not a matter of being right or wrong but principals and department heads need information to make right decisions. The principal or department head should be thoroughly briefed on the problem, including steps taken by the counselor. Every effort should be made not only to give the background information to the problem, but a detailed explanation of the strategies that have been undertaken. In so doing the principal and department head gain further insights into the problem and have more information upon which to make their decision.

Departmental Directives

There are times when academic department heads will issue a directive to the counselors to make certain level changes for students. These should be noted in the counselor's "Follow Up" file. (See Chapter 17, Follow up File) Rarely is the follow up not executed. When it is not, the counselor is at fault. However, it is still incumbent on the department head to check that the directive has been executed. When it concerns a schedule change initiated by the department head, he/she should notify his/her staff of the impending change. Teachers should report back when the change has not taken place. In a word, not all the blame should be laid at the counselor's doorstep. Simply to issue the request, forget about it and say that the counselor is at fault, can also be a cover up for poor administrative follow through.

A Unique Kind of Academic Recognition Ceremony

There are a number of ceremonies to recognize high achieving students for their academic and or athletic achievements. Rarely are students struggling to rise above failing grades recognized for their achievement. A small private recognition ceremony in the principal's office is an ideal way to recognize these students. Since the principal and counselor are dealing with marginal students who may slip back into failure, it is best to keep the ceremony simple and private. The best time for this is after the first semester. If the guidance department and the principal accept the concept, a set procedure should be in place to achieve this goal.

1. The first step in the process is to canvass fellow counselors for the names of any students who have made a real effort to succeed and have risen from being failing students to ones who have made real progress.

2. Once the list has been compiled, the counselors should review the cumulative list to make sure that none of these students have difficulties elsewhere (attendance, discipline, in class misconduct, etc.) Since some of these students might cause embarrassment to the principal, they should not be invited to the ceremony. However, their passing grades should be recognized and students encouraged by the counselor in a counseling session.

3. For those who are invited, a nicely prepared invitation should be sent to these students requesting their presence in the principal's office on a specific day and time. Although this invitation may be simple, it is valued highly by these students and shared with their parents. Unlike many high-powered students, this could easily be the first time they are in the principal's office for any anything other than discipline.

4. Keeping the ceremony relatively private in the principal's office safeguards all involved should a student have a relapse in either conduct or academic performance. The **hope** is that the ceremony will provide impetus for continued success.

A Suggestion for Administrators

Throughout this handbook are multiple programs and practices for counselors: a program for college dropout prevention, special nights for ELL students and their parents, inspirational quotes for the P.A. system, motivational use of the principal's office, a recognition ceremony for students making academic strides from failing to passing, etc. **They are not the sole providence of the counseling department.** If for legitimate reasons the guidance department cannot sponsor such programs, administrators with their resources should consider sponsoring them.

*"In adversity, man is saved by **hope**." Menanderer*
(As recommended by Barbara Mullins)

Special Arrangements

Some principals make special, justifiable arrangements or promises to parents or students but forget to inform the counselor of his/her part in the arrangement. The counselor should be informed and on board with the special arrangement. In this way, there will be no foul ups and the counselor will not be caught in an embarrassing situation.

The Righteous Administrator

Generally speaking, administrators and department heads are very thorough but they do occasionally make mistakes. Fortunately, for them, they are not subject to the same kind of scrutiny as counselors. Their mistakes, such as insufficient familiarity with certain board policies or state regulations, or making decisions on insufficient information, can be quietly swept under the carpet. Sadly, some administrators will come down very hard on staff and counselors making the very same mistakes. This is not to say that accountability should not be in place, especially for frequent counselor mistakes, but it should have some degree of understanding for the hard working counselor.

Administrative Unawareness

It is unfortunate when some administrators do not rise up through ranks and have no real understanding of what really goes on in the guidance office. Although some may have had a cordial and even a good working relationship with counselors, an in-depth knowledge of the counselor's workload and responsibilities is lacking. As a result, some administrators do not fully understand the flow of guidance services in the course of an academic year. When things are running smoothly and problems are not arriving at the administrator's door, the work of the counselor is usually taken for granted. However, once there is a complaint, the administrator arrives at the counselor's door. How often do they arrive when things are going smoothly?

Case Study

A case in point is graduation time. Some students do not meet graduation requirements. If the parents have been notified well in advance and conferences are held, there are no complaints. Graduation comes off without a hitch because the counselor has done his/her job, often at considerable time-consuming expense with both the student and the parents. Seldom do administrators realize this and even more seldom do they express their satisfaction after graduation for a job well done. How many are the students that graduate who got there through the incessant efforts of the counselor over a four-year period? However, for a student not to graduate and the parents not forewarned, there are legitimate grounds for a complaint. This represents a real thorn in the principal's side and there will be repercussions...rightly so. However, when things go well there is no harm in recognizing the work of the counselors.

Administrative Sensitivity

At times when administrators receive parental letters of commendation for counselors, they are not even mentioned to the counselor. It seems administrators have a defensive approach to praising individuals and passing along this information to the counselor. Is this for fear that at some future date, they might be quoted?

Concern for Foreign Born Students

There are multiple concerns for which administrators should demonstrate interest. One such concern should be the proper placement, adjustment, and acceptance into the school community of foreign-born students, which is vital to their success. In some schools, this concern is not fully demonstrated. In these cases, the role of the counselor should be:

1. **To assist administrators in becoming aware of any failings in the admissions process of ELL students.**

2. **To invite administrators to various ELL (English Language Learners) functions**

3. To encourage special visits by the principal to ELL classes.

Orientation of New Counselors

Whether a counselor is new to the job or is experienced and taking someone's place, it is a disservice to students that administrators do not provide a **real guidance orientation to new counselors.** Just to have a general get together with new staff, or an hour's meeting with the department head is not enough to understand adequately the nature of each school's guidance program. Since the counselor is dealing with human beings: students, parents, teachers and administrators, an orientation pertaining to each are required to avoid the most common pitfalls. School policies pertaining to guidance must be reviewed. The intricacies of scheduling, record keeping, and individual assignments must be clearly understood. Learning as you go along is to invite mistakes usually at the expense of the student. To avoid such problems, administrators must plan extensive guidance orientations for new counselors. Do not throw them to the lions. For sure, the counselor's mistakes will come back to haunt the administrator.

"Uneasy is the head that wears a crown." Shakespeare (As suggested by Michael Leonard)

CHAPTER 5

Guidance and Teachers

Tech teacher, Mr. Jack Murrin, and student, Leland Murdock

A Team Approach

Perhaps the greatest need for a team approach to helping students is that between the counselor and the teacher. Most student academic and social problems center in the classroom or gym. Academic failures, in-class discipline problems, and students who are rejected by their peers require joint communication between counselor and teacher. Of all school personnel, the counselor deals most with the teaching staff. The information related here represents just a small segment of all that pertains to teachers. Information contained in the chapters for parents, counselors, and administrators also applies to the teacher. The classroom teacher is the heart of the building, and hence the teacher–counselor relationship is crucial. So much good can come out of a fine working relationship, such as the following:

1. Counselors are immediately notified of students falling apart
2. Special arrangements are made to assist students in meeting their obligations
3. Difficult parents are handled as a team
4. Counselor or teacher mistakes are handled as colleagues and not as adversaries
5. Lines of communication are frequent and direct
6. Collegial arrangements are made to assist each other in dealing with other problems: parent complaints, student placement, parental notifications, etc.
7. There is mutual sharing regarding the well being of students
8. Etc.

Setting up Teacher Conferences

A convenient way to maximize staff attendance at a parent/teachers conference is to schedule it for the last period in the day. Some teachers are free for that period and those teachers who have class are invited to join in immediately after school. Any teacher who cannot attend both parts is given the parents' phone number and urged to contact them as soon as possible. Early morning conferences are good but are cut short by the beginning of the first period, and teachers with classes the first two periods cannot make it.

Notify Teachers

When setting up a meeting with teachers and parents, always be sure on the day of the meeting to re-notify the teachers. Nothing is more embarrassing than to schedule a parent/teachers meeting and no or few teachers show up. Request that teachers, who cannot make it, notify the counselor so that the parents may be told at the meeting. Likewise, teachers should indicate when they **will** call the parents. This procedure should be worked out with the guidance secretaries so that much of the mechanical work is in place.

Teacher Changes

When parents ask for a teacher change, always contact the teacher to get the other side of the story and have the teacher aware of the situation. This helps to avoid hard feelings and poor teacher relations. Encourage the teacher to make contact with the parent to work out the problem.

At Opposite Ends

In some schools, counselors and physical education teachers seem to be at odds. This is a pity since one of the major obstacles to graduation is the failure of students to meet graduation P.E. requirements. A good working relationship with P.E. teachers brings about mutual sharing of information. In one instance, the P.E. teacher may advocate for tutorial help for a student. On the other, the counselor may share mitigating circumstances with regard to a specific student. In no way, may state regulations be circumvented. However, there are creative ways to help students to meet state P.E. requirements.

In some school situations, P.E. teachers pride themselves on the fact that they help more students get into college than the counselors. The fact that they are in such a unique relationship with students is laudable. However, how much more could be done for more students if there were a team effort on both sides!

P.E. Staff

The need for a good working relationship with the P.E. staff cannot be stressed sufficiently! They of all staff members see students in a different environment, which reveals students' character, physical condition, and ability to relate to peers. Moreover, many of the P.E. staff are school coaches and have contact with parents. The amount of information they accumulate can be very helpful to the counselor. Additionally, some have an even greater influence over students than the counselor has and can assist in bringing about change.

Case Study

In the course of a school year, P.E. teachers, just by observing, have related the following potential problems to counselors for their follow up:

1. Kids with all the symptoms of drug abuse or alcoholism, some confirmed by classmates friendly to the coach.
2. Girls throwing up in the locker room who are bulimic
3. Kids undernourished
4. Kids who are embarrassed by their body parts
5. Kids who are anti-social
6. Bullies, loners, hostile and angry students
7. Etc.

P.E. Changes

In the matter of scheduling physical education changes, there are usually large numbers in these classes. Many changes are generated at the beginning of the year and semester turn over. As a matter of courtesy and for student accountability, it is recommended that the P.E. teachers be notified directly of a change the counselor makes. The system may not be computerized and because of large class numbers, the P.E. teachers greatly appreciate the notice. Likewise, counselors should be notified if a P.E. teacher switches a student from one section to another.

Convoluted P.E. Requirements

In some school districts, physical education courses are divided into quarters, semesters, etc. If students fail one of these, they are required to double up the next or, more confusing, to make up parts of a failed course the next quarter, etc. It becomes even more confusing when at the end of the quarter, etc. a student receives an incomplete and there is a private arrangement with the P.E. teacher to make up the work missing. What does the counselor do? Schedule the student for a make up or wait and see? If the student does not complete the make up, will it be too late to reschedule the student? Additionally, some students consistently fail physical education for a number of reasons. Gradually, this accumulates to a significant amount of record keeping and confusion. Unclear procedures and arrangements put a strain on the counselor and P.E. teacher relationship. Who is responsible for what? What procedures are to be followed? Since in most districts a requisite number of physical education credits are required for graduation, a simple and clear system to make sure that all requirements are met must be worked out by an administrator and the physical education coordinator to avoid all the above complications.

Red Alert!

In the course of working with parents, there may be occasions where parents are angry at the school system. Some of their children have been bounced around from school to school, or treated poorly by teachers, counselors or administrators. As a result, some parents feel that they may not have received a fair deal. When dealing with school personnel, they may become hostile and vindictive. This usually occurs when they are unfamiliar with state regulations or are trying to circumvent them. It is extremely important that the counselor fully apprises the parent of state regulations. Should the parent be trying to put pressure on the teacher of record, the teacher should be alerted to the situation so as not to be sandbagged when confronting the parent.

Case Study

In the case of a young woman who attended several schools, her physical education requirements were not up to date. The parent viewed this as a non-issue and asked that accommodations be made for the student to graduate anyway. The counselor informed the parent that state regulations applied and there could be no waiver for the requirement. The parent immediately requested an appointment be set up with the head of the physical education department. Before the meeting, the counselor went to the chairperson, explained not only the educational background of the student but also the angry disposition of the parent. The counselor alerted him that he would have a fight on his hands. A nasty fight did ensue, but at least the chairperson was forewarned and was prepared to deal with the parent. Such instances as this also apply when parents may be angry with a classroom teacher or physical education teacher.

How to Handle Difficult Teacher Changes

Most schools do not allow counselors to change teachers when requested by a parent or student. If a student comes to see the counselor and the counselor knows that the answer is "NO," then say simply, "NO." However, as you speak to the student, privately make a quick search of the student's schedule. It may reveal that a change is not **physically possible**. If this is the case, tell the student that it is also physically impossible to make the change. The student will then feel that you made an effort and in a sense, it is the student's decision to remain with that teacher. If this method is not feasible, a detailed explanation of school policy is in order. This method also allows the students to see that the counselor is concerned and trying to help. It is also advisable to recommend a source of tutoring for any student in danger of failing.

Teacher Files

When dealing with teachers and matters of significance, the counselor should keep a teacher file and add notes to his/her file. This procedure is also recommended for teachers as part of their student records to assist in solving problems. This is especially important when dealing with administrators to substantiate the teacher's and counselor's position or to make a point with the administration or parent. This practice will either benefit the teacher or document a negative special circumstance.

Liberal Attitude

Teachers with a liberal attitude toward attendance in a study hall do a disservice to students who frequently cut. These students know that they can take liberties and get away with cutting the study hall. This not only encourages bad habits but also frees students to be somewhere in the building where they may cause a disturbance.

Not on Time for Class

Teachers, who have a policy of locking their door when the bell rings, are obviously teaching students to be on time. However, if the student has to get a pass to re-enter, as much as twenty minutes of instructional time is lost before the student can get a signed pass. A clever student who wants to cut the class can wait until the period is almost over and then return to class. Provision has to be made so that lost instructional time does not occur. This also works in reverse. If the teacher is frequently late, students will gage their arrival accordingly.

"A teacher affects eternity;
He can never tell where
His influence stops." Henry B. Adams (As researched by Jeanette and Marie Murtha)

CHAPTER 6

Guidance and the Special Education Student

****

There is no picture inserted here, because a picture cannot identify special education children. They are no different from other children, except they learn differently.

****

A Life-long Struggle

In dealing with parents of children with learning disabilities or other educationally impairing problems, it is well to remember that for their parents it is life-long struggles to assist their children achieve their full potential. Along with this struggle come the personal feelings of parents. They feel a sense of deprivation and sorrow that their child will have to go through life with a disability. Some have feelings of guilt. Most parents accept the challenge. They will do all in their power to see that their children receive the services that they rightfully deserve. Some parents, understandably, become overly aggressive in their effort, which is to their credit, but are, nonetheless, difficult with which to deal. Counselors and teachers should keep in mind the underlying motivation of these parents is the good of the child. In working with all parents of special education children, counselors and teachers need to be both patient and understanding of the special needs of these children and the concerns of the parents.

Equally Admirable

The admiration and respect that teachers and counselors should have for the parents of learning disabled youngsters may be equally applied to their children. How edifying it is to see the extraordinary efforts put forth by the youngsters who are trying to learn and succeed! What takes some students minutes to learn, may take them hours. Day after day, month after month, and year after year, they persevere in their struggle. The fact should not be lost sight of that their disability poses an overwhelming obstacle to surmount.

Gold is tried by fire, brave men by adversity." Seneca
(As suggested by librarian, Virginia Harley)

The Challenge

Special education is a challenging and complicated field. At times, the special education department can be at odds with the guidance department. The main area of contention is accountability.

Who is responsible for a particular service?

Who issues the SSD form (Services for Students with Disabilities) to parents?

Who is responsible for notifying parents that it will take six weeks or longer before approval of the SSD accommodations are granted?

Who is responsible for notifying teachers that a new student in their class receives accommodations and which ones?

When there is a schedule change, who is responsible for notifying the teacher of the student's accommodations?

These issues and many more must be worked out, systematically, by the department heads in each school. If procedures are not set in place and are not clearly defined then students will be affected negatively and the guidance-special education relationships strained.

Request for Special Education Placement

Any request for Special Education Placement must be referred first to the Special Education Coordinator who will determine the procedure to be followed.

The Special Education Teachers

In dealing with special education students, the learning disabilities teacher must be the most sensitive. They become involved with students and know their educational limitations. It is a challenge to deal with the mind and emotions of these young students. In addition, the learning specialist has time to share experiences with these students in and out the classroom. Consequently, a real bond develops between the student and the teacher and amazing results are achieved. On the other hand, when no special concern or serious instruction is delivered, a disservice is done to these students. Admittedly, some special education students are very difficult to deal with both from a disciplinary and emotional point of view. This relates to the fact that many classified students may have a poor self-concept due to their disability. Many stories could be told, as in Chapter 2, of the atrocities these youngsters perform on themselves to relieve their personal pain, from self-mutilation to suicide. More likely than not, theses youngsters will act out in some subtle way to express their frustration. Hence, the role of the learning specialist is so weighty and crucial. These teachers are neither psychologists nor therapists, but they are caring professionals who make a difference.

Psychological Services

Whenever parents request psychological testing, they must submit a "Permission to Test" form to the school psychologist. Whenever counselors are asked to release confidential information, a signed release form must be submitted by the parents to the person in charge of sending out this information.

IEP and Psychological Release

Whenever the counselor is processing a college application for a special education student that requires an IEP and a psychological report, the counselor must have on file a parental permission to release all such information

Social Services

When students require certain social services, they should be referred to the school social worker, if there is one. The social worker may also serve in the capacity of a Drug and Alcohol Coordinator.

There are times when home visits are required. The social worker may be required to investigate child abuse circumstances. Likewise, the social worker should provide information and assistance in obtaining social services for students depending on the circumstances of the student.

Special Education Documentation

Any transferring Special Education student entering the building should have all pertinent documents, including an IEP (Individual Education Plan) and the results of psychological testing. Receiving schools have the right to this information, but it is best to work with the parents in obtaining it. **(See Addendum 11, Family Educational Rights and Privacy Act.)** It is best to have the parents sign a release form requesting that this information be sent. Some schools will not allow transferring students to enter the building without first presenting these documents. It is very difficult to place such a student without pertinent information. At registration, the appropriate secretary should inform these parents that all pertinent documents must be in place before registering.

Change of Placement

The Committee of Special Education places all Special Education Students. Therefore, counselors cannot honor a request from a parent or a teacher for a change of placement without approval from the C.S.E. Nor can the counselor make a change of schedule that affects the IEP without the approval of the special education coordinator, and the committee if necessary.

Course Changes for Special Education Students

When there is a course change during the year in a special education student's schedule, the new teacher must receive a copy of the student's IEP. The counselor should send a copy of the course change to the special education coordinator so that the IEP can be forwarded

In this way, all the accommodations will be put in place.

Case Study

A young man was placed by the CSE in an out of district school. He had all the rights and privileges of returning to the high school for graduation. His mother requested that the counselor gather information on her son's senior photo, cap and gown, all dates for graduation rehearsal and to make sure that his proper name appears on his diploma. The counselor, because the student was special ed., assumed this was his job. So he took it upon himself to supply all the information. Collecting this information was time consuming. As it turned out the initial parental request was too late for both the graduation pictures and the placement of his name in the high school program. The parent was outraged and blamed the counselor. Had the counselor initially referred the parent to the proper personnel, he/she would not have had to endure the blame for the late notices, despite his/her good intentions. (**See Addendum 3.**) Matters of this nature should be discussed at the CSE meeting to avoid future complications.

SSD (Services for Students with Disabilities) Form

When counselors are registering a new high school student who is classified, the counselor should notify and send all documents to the director of special education. He/she, in turn, should get back to the counselor and recommend course placements. If the student has not done so, the parent should fill out a SSD form that is required for accommodations on standardized tests (PSAT, SAT, etc.) If the student intends to take the ACT, the ACT has its own form for accommodations and should be filed well in advance.

Advising Parents

Counselors should know who is responsible for notifying parents of special education procedures, especially when they are requesting classification of their child or in high school filing the SSD accommodation form for standardized SAT/ACT tests. Failure to follow the procedure may result in the student not receiving the accommodations on time for the test. This can be a real public relations nightmare or possibly require a derogatory letter placed in a counselor's file. More astonishingly, it could become a real "head hunting" episode leading to non-tenure. A worthwhile procedure is that when a student is classified or designated as 504, the parents should be given the SSD form on the spot and asked to fill it out and sign it. Then whoever is responsible for filling out the rest of the document can do so and send it out immediately. In the end, an administrator must sign off on the document, before it is sent. In cases where a special education student is entering the high school for the first time, the form should be given when the special education coordinator verifies the classification. When eighth graders are entering the ninth, the coordinator of the special education program should have a procedure worked out for filling out the required forms. In some schools, the guidance department is charged with this responsibility. Whoever it might be, the procedure should be in place.

Anecdote

One summer, the deadline date for requesting approval for accommodations from the SSD for the PSAT occurred in August, well before most students had returned to school.

Someone should have been responsible for notifying the parents of this date, so that the application could be filed on time. A significant amount of students missed the deadline and had to take the PSAT under normal testing conditions, without accommodations. Who was at fault? What procedures should have been set in place to avoid such a travesty?

SAT—Electronic Applications

Special Education students who file to take the SAT's on line should be reminded that their **SSD number** should be included, if they wish to receive accommodations. This number is found in the letter of notification from the College Board granting accommodations.

SAT Standby Testing for Learning Disabled Students

If classified students intend to take the SAT, etc., they have to file their SSD identification number with the regular application at the appropriate time. If they miss the deadline and wish to take the SAT as a standby, it will be denied. Because advanced arrangements are required, students requiring accommodations cannot test as standbys. There is insufficient time to set up the special arrangements for their accommodations.

Important!

If a student has SSD clearance for accommodations **and another accommodation is added by the CSE,** the new accommodation must be approved by the SSD by submitting the **"Add Accommodation"** form. Failure to file will not include the new accommodation in taking the SAT, AP, etc.

Teacher Notification

Simply to assume that once a student has been classified by the CSE that all accommodations will be afforded the student, is incorrect. Each year at the beginning of the term, after a reasonable amount of time has passed, parents should check that their student's teachers have been notified of the accommodations on the IEP.

Challenging an IEP

In the legal controversy over who bears the burden of proof when a request is made for a radical change in the IEP, such as a change of school placement, the U.S. Supreme Court ruled that the burden of proof lies with the party seeking relief. If the parent requests the change, the burden is on the parent. If the school district challenges an IEP, it is obligated to supply the proof. Parents will now have to be more zealous and proof driven in their efforts to change the placement of their children because of this ruling.

Special Education and Homebound Instruction

If a student receives resource room services in school, he/she should also receive these services during homebound instruction. Any provision for extended time, etc., is applicable in home instruction. This may require additional time beyond the normal two hours per day recommended by New York State.

Special Education Students and Summer School

If a special education student fails a course and intends to attend summer school, the special education coordinator or the counselor should notify the summer school administrator regarding the IEP accommodations for each student on a separate summer school form. This is usually done when the student comes to the counselor to sign up for summer school.

GED

Students, who are classified and wish to receive accommodations for their GED test, should obtain the form L-15 and send it to the N.Y. State special education GED administrator. Each state has its own procedure for this. Counselors should be aware that it is a special circumstance.

College Bound Special Education Students

For special education students interested in attending college, the home school counselor is not responsible for the implementation of 504 or IEP accommodations at the college level. These students have to file for accommodations with the college special support department and supply current testing before the college semester begins. Additionally, colleges are looking for students who can advocate for themselves. Their learning specialist teacher in high school should instruct each student how to explain their learning style and how to advocate for their special accommodations.

Triennials

When students submit their college application and request a placement in a learning disabilities support program, colleges require recent psychological testing that cannot be more than a year old. The triennial, therefore, should take place in the junior year, and be ready for submission early in the senior year. Be aware that colleges are more and more demanding that the learning disability be fully documented and within the norms required for classification. **Marginal classifications may be considered invalid** and the student denied services.

Counselor Guidelines for LD Students Preparing to Attend College

In the college admissions process, the counselor should remind the student to:

1. Check with the high school's special education department that all the accommodations are listed on the IEP and are up to date.

2. Make sure he/she has filed the application for accommodations with the college support department in advance of the college deadline date.

3. In addition to the regular admissions officer, set up an appointment with the director of the college support program to learn about the services offered.

4. Visit the college's learning support center.

5. Talk to other students in the college's support program to gain insights and to evaluate the program.

6. Understand, that for most colleges, the student must be accepted in the regular admissions process before he/she can be accepted into the college support program.

Accommodations in the Senior Year

Counselors should advise parents that if they are requesting a special education classification or 504 designation for their son or daughter in their senior year, they should do so as soon as possible. Once classified, they should file the SSD form. It will take at least six to eight weeks before they will be cleared to take the first SAT with accommodations in their senior year. This will bring them past the first ACT, SAT test dates. The College Board is leery of giving accommodations to students whose learning disabilities have just been diagnosed in the senior year. Hence, the long advance registration and the need for a well-documented classification.

Selecting the Right College L. D. Support Program

Below are three types of programs offered to LD students by colleges. Both the student and the parent, in conjunction with the student's learning specialist, should determine which is the most appropriate.

Type A

1. Tutorial services that are offered not by a learning specialist but by professors, graduate students or peer tutors who will attempt to remediate learning problems.

2. The instructors assisting students in Type A are not trained learning specialists.

3. These services may also include developmental centers in study skills, math, reading, and English, offered to all students.

4. Open to all with no extra fee.

Type B

1. Tutorial services that are directed toward LD students to assist them with their course work

2. Included in the services may be assistance in obtaining texts on tape, untimed tests, oral exams, taped lectures, note copiers, and proof reading help, etc.

3. Instructional assistance may or may not necessarily be given by a learning specialist and is open to LD students. Generally, there is no fee.

4. To obtain these services the student has to be proactive, identify his /her learning disability with documentation, and be in contact with the support program director so that professors will be notified of accommodations.

5. The student, each semester, must request that professors be notified of his/her accommodations.

Type C

1. A specific learning disabilities program is offered, which provides a trained learning specialist who works directly with the LD student in a mandated, structured program.

2. The services include all of Type B (tutorials, accommodations, etc.) plus counseling and training in coping and self-advocacy skills and administered by a learning specialist.

3. Open only to LD students and requires a special application and an additional fee.

4. The program director will automatically notify the professors each semester of the student's accommodations.

Parents and students, with the help of the school learning specialist, have to determine:

1. Which **type** of service meets the student's needs

2. If the services are actually in place at the college

Parents and students should be aware of the possibility that colleges may offer only some of the services listed. The availability of all such services should be checked out in advance. A diligent search will determine what **TYPE** best meets the student's college needs.

Preventing College Drop Outs

In **Chapter 18** on College Planning is a program for preventing college dropouts. One of the major concerns regarding special education students when they get to college is that they could easily become discouraged. Having a mentor who is not a parent and who follows the plan as outlined will be a great assistance to such a student. For a concerned parent, it need not be part of a school program and can be set up independently by the parent.

RICHARD O'CONNELL, ED. D.

Creative Solutions to College Requirements

Students, who have waivers in their IEP for a foreign language in high school or have a documented severe learning disability in math, may have to take a foreign language or math courses in college. These could pose real obstacles in meeting graduation requirements. However, if the student or parent is in contact with the director of the learning support program in college, special arrangement may be worked out to solve the dilemma. Requirements are not usually waived in college. However, substitutions may be approved. Courses within the curriculum of the foreign language department may be substituted. If approved, foreign films in a foreign language with English subtitles may be used. Courses in computers may be substituted for a math course. These are examples and the solution will lie in the creativity of the director of the learning support program. A word of caution for New York State residents is that six credits in a foreign language and math are required for a New York State teacher's certification, with not substitution of courses recognized.

A Good Idea

There are some colleges, which insist that if a student is to enter their learning support program that there be a relative living nearby. This is to assure that if the student has emotional or academic problems, encouragement from family is nearby in time of need. Each parent knows the strengths and weakness of his/her son or daughter. This will be a determining factor in selecting the location and choice of the college support program. It is naive for some parents or students to think there will be a radical change for the better when the student goes off to college. In fact, given the distractions of college life, it is even more difficult than high school. Assume that if a student needs support in high school, they will definitely need assistance in college. Not to do so is a serious mistake.

Knowing the College Rights of Learning Disabled Students

The U.S. Department of Education has prepared a document that specifically refers to the rights of learning disabled students at the post secondary level:

Students with Disabilities Preparing for Postsecondary Education:
Know Your Rights and Responsibilities
U.S. Department of Education

A copy of this document may be found in **Addendum 9.**

Some Tips for College Bound Learning Disabled Students

1. Generally, students who have a learning disability, must first apply for regular admission To apply to a learning support program in college is not an automatic acceptance into college.

2. Students with Learning Disabilities should know their learning style and be able to explain their learning disability to college admissions and support personnel. In this way, the students will be given information on the college's support services that specifically apply to them. It is very important that college support programs meet the student's needs. Additionally, admissions and support personnel are impressed when a student can articulate his/her needs. This skill can only take place if the parent, and especially the learning specialist, require their students to know their learning disabilities and guide them in articulating how they learn.

3. If a college cannot supply the support services needed by the student, look elsewhere. Parents and resource room teachers play a key role in evaluating college services. Many L.D. students under assess the assistance they will need in college.

4. Importantly, L.D. students should be trained in self-advocacy skills. They must **seek** out the help they need while at college. If required accommodations are not afforded, they must alert the support personnel

in charge to supply them or notify their professors to implement the accommodations. Students who are not trained to be assertive in making sure their accommodations are in place will find it very difficult to succeed in college.

5. Parents and counselors are to make sure that the student's IEP and psychological documents are recent and sent to the appropriate college office when requested.

6. Students should always have a copy in their personal file of their **final exit IEP and psy.** If they are not given, it is their right to have them. Request them. Give a photocopy to college support personnel. The student may need other copies for graduate school or to apply for accommodations on graduate standardized tests.

7. Transition plans for exiting seniors are the new thrust in IEP planning from New York State. The guidance counselor will be an integral part of this plan. It may have as many as 10 pages of narratives detailing specifics about the student's learning style, testing, and future plans and will include many of the ideas stated above. **(See Chapter 18** for more information on the college application process.)

Graduation Requirements, Curriculum Handbook and Competency Exams.

The advice given to interns and beginning counselor applies here to parents of classified students. As advocates for their children, parents must know the graduation requirements, the exceptions for special education children and the special services offered to assist their children to meet these requirements.

Suspended Special Education Students

Each suspended special education student is eligible for home instruction to the extent indicated in the IEP. Under normal circumstances, the New York State requires two hours a day. However, to meet the needs of the student, more time may be required. The help of the Director of Special Education may be needed in such cases. Realistically, the school should provide services within a few days. If it takes longer, lost days may be made up.

Out of District Students

Many out of district students are special education students who need a different educational environment to succeed. Whatever the cause of their placement, many feel alienated from their home school. Counselors are encouraged to keep in contact with these students so they have a sense of belonging and that someone in their home school cares for them.

"The bravest sight in all the world is a man (woman) fighting against the odds." Franklin K. Lane
(As attributed to Claire Donnelly, Dolores Prior, Brendan Loonam, Paula Caravelli and Kathleen Maura Quinn)

CHAPTER 7

Guidance and the Foreign Born Student

Pictured above are English Language Learners, a member of the International Club wearing a traditional Portuguese costume and their moderator-counselor at a welcoming dinner for ELL students and parents.

Sponsor Special Events

The counselor of ELL students and staff members who work with ELL students should consider sponsoring an event for foreign-born students and their parents. Such events as a welcoming ceremony, a brunch or a get together night, make foreign-born students and their families feel part of the school community and less isolated. At such events, the foreign-born families usually extend themselves and make a significant contribution of food. An invitation should be extended to the faculty to attend as well. Their students welcome the faculty's generous participation and it is an opportunity for parents to meet staff. Parents of ELL students are reluctant to attend formal teacher meetings because of their language barrier.

We Are All Children of Immigrants

In admitting new foreign-born students into the building, it is well for the counselors and teachers to remind themselves that we are all children of immigrants who came to America to better the lives of their children. We are the result of their sacrifice and hard work. We have the privilege of helping these young children to become the productive, taxpaying citizens of the future. Let us make sure that these new immigrants do not suffer the alienation and degradation our fore parents suffered. There is a tradition in many schools of acceptance and nurturing of these students who are experiencing real cultural adjustment. Some of these children are parents themselves or have come from very limited educational backgrounds and are heroic in their efforts to succeed. They need encouragement and support. The counselor should put them on his/her "at risk" list so as not to forget them.

Nomenclature

The acronyms for students coming from a foreign country who are learning English are multiple: ELL (English Language Learners), ESL (English as a Second Language), ESOL (English Speakers of Another Language), etc. For purposes of consistency, the acronym ELL will be used and it is meant to incorporate the others.

Keep in Contact

When registering foreign-born students, follow school procedures. Try to keep in contact with these children. Find out what classrooms they are in and pop in occasionally. Aside from their classroom teachers, the counselor may be the only other school official they will know or be able to recognize.

Grading ELL Students

Beginning counselors and teachers should know the school's policy on grading English Language Learners. Part of the orientation of new teachers should be that they are informed of the grading policy for ELL students. There are usually three levels of grading:

1. Audit
2. Pass/Fail
3. Normal grading

The ELL coordinator will determine at what level ELL students should be graded. A memo has to be sent to each teacher clarifying how the student is to be graded.

Financial Aid for ELL Students

In assisting ELL students to obtain financial aid for college, the counselor must be aware of their immigration status. Knowing the state and federal guidelines for receiving financial aid is an asset in assisting ELL students. No financial aid is afforded these students unless their immigration status meets the state and federal guidelines.

Admitting and Grade Recording for ELL Students

When foreign-born students arrive in the United States, many come without academic records. A procedure should be in place for their assessment and placement. Some of these children may be in their teens with a limited educational background. There are instances where these youngsters have been working in fields just a few days before arriving in the counselor's office. Their proper placement **is crucial** so that they experience some success. As time goes by, easy money at a mundane job, which leads to nowhere, will tempt them to leave school. It is important that they have some sense of **success** and direction in school in order to prevent an early drop out.

Case Study

An eighteen-year-old ELL student was placed in ninth grade classes based on her age and assumed capabilities in the hope she might graduate. She was not properly assessed and even the ninth grade level was beyond her capacity. She became frustrated, discouraged, and dropped out of school. In reality, the young lady had little educational training and was in over her head. In addition, there was very little likelihood that she could meet all the requirements for graduation by the age of twenty-one. **She was poorly placed.** A better placement would have been a referral to an adult ELL program wherein the goal of a GED would be a greater reality. All too often, this type of student is placed and then forgotten about until he/she drops out.

Team Work

A counselor's close working relationship with the ELL teacher or coordinator is most beneficial. The coordinator, after testing the student's English and math skills, should recommend to the counselor the proper grade level, ELL classes and additional courses the student should be taking. The counselor, guided by this knowledge, can supplement the student's schedule with other electives as well as placing him/her with nurturing teachers.

Interesting Electives

When the counselor thinks of the kind of day ELL students have, filled with drills and rote learning, it must not only be boring but also mentally exhausting for them. To supply these students with a happy and practical experience during the day is a real gift to these students. There are electives for boys and girls, which are hands on, require minimal English skills, and lead to productive careers. These should be chosen.

Know Your Staff

Simply to place a student into a class without considering the teacher is a disservice to ELL students. These students require more work and a greater degree of acceptance. Choose teachers, where possible, who are understanding and accepting.

Don't Fall Prey

In schools, some staff members are biased to incoming foreign-born students. They forget their own heritage and complain that their tax money is paying for these foreigners. Every effort has to be made by the counselor to champion the benefits of educating foreign-born students. Where possible, students should not be placed in such teachers classes.

Pliable

When ELL students arrive on the counselor's doorstep, they are usually quite innocent, pliable, and willing to learn. At this point, most ELL students have not been tainted by their new environment and affected by the rough element in which they may be placed. It is a wonderful opportunity for the school community to extend warmth and concern. These students are open to values and the need to be good citizens. This is a weighty responsibility placed on the school community, but one that offers a challenge and a privilege.

Sponsoring Career Education

With the realization that some foreign-born students will age out before they can receive a diploma, career plans should be set in place for these students. In most districts, they have occupational training schools and these students should be directed to these schools to learn a lifetime trade wherein they can support themselves. (See Chapter 28 on Career Planning)

Keep in Touch

The one thing that foreign-born students need is constant reassurance and recognition. A counselor cannot devote all his time to this effort but the concept of being in the halls at key times, even for a few minutes, will afford the counselor opportunities of just saying hello to passing ELL students.

Isolation

When youngsters feel isolated, they tend to gather around those they know. In this case, it is other foreign-born students. As a result, they become more and more isolated. In conjunction with the ELL staff, every effort should be made by the counselor to get these youngsters to join clubs, sports, and activities that bring them into meaningful contact with their other school peers. Soccer, for example, is usually a sport where foreign-born students are welcomed and accepted as peers by their teammates.

ELL Students and Special Education Placement

To determine if an ELL student needs special education services, the student must be tested in her/his native language by a qualified psychologist who also is fluent in the student's language. This service is usually provided by BOCES or another outside testing agency. However, a real distinction must be made between the student who is limited by a new language that is preventing him/her from learning and, in addition to the language barrier, there is the possibility of a learning disability. Consequently, a cautious approach must be taken to determine the real cause before attempting to classify an ELL student.

Recognize a Pattern of Absenteeism

The backgrounds of some of the ELL students include poverty, and in some case little parental support from home. Whenever there is a pattern of absences, it indicates that the above causes may be at the heart of the problem, other than illness. This is a dangerous pattern because it indicates a problem that could lead to dropping out. As much intervention as possible, including all support services, should be set in motion. It is the job of the counselor to recognize the problem, and provide as much intervention and support as possible.

Case Study

The counselor in charge of ELL students observed such a pattern of absences, as mentioned above. It was decided that the counselor with the social worker should pay a visit to the home of the truant young lady. The student was at home... tending to her sick one-year-old child and could not come to school. In addition, it was learned that the young woman had a part time job. The grandmother would mind the infant while she went to work at night. To the young woman's credit, she had enough intelligence to realize that she, as well as her child, would not have a productive life unless she finished high school. With the aid of the social worker, plans were made to get the infant medical care and childcare support while the mother attended high school.

Need for Translators

Not all counselors can speak several languages to meet the needs of ELL students. The services of a translator or faculty member, fluent in the student's native language, should be set in place to facilitate communication. Both the director of guidance and the ELL coordinator should initiate this service according to union and school guidelines.

The same holds true for letters, announcements, and reports sent home to parents or guardians. In schools with a large ELL population, official letters and news briefs should be sent home in translation to keep the ELL community informed.

Translating Documents

Of special difficulty for counselors are the tasks of:
1. Translating foreign documents
2. Figuring out the grade level appropriate to the document
3. The titles of courses
4. And the equivalent grades.

These guidelines must come from the principal and board policy. However, they may not all be in place because of the unique country that the student comes from. In these cases, a set procedure should be agreed upon by the administration to expedite the entrance of foreign-born students into the school. It is shameful when students are kept waiting days on end to be admitted to class.

"Foreigners are contemporary prosperity." Madame de Stall
(As suggested by Heather Rugel)

CHAPTER 8

Guidance and Staff Relations

Case Study

Usually a topic is introduced by some other means than a **case study**. However, in this instance, the importance of a good working relationship with staff is best orchestrated by a case study.

Every school may have one or two teachers who do not get the job done. They are incompetent, sarcastic, vengeful, or burned out. This kind of teacher can really hurt children, especially if they manage to have all four components of failure. (This is not to say that counselors can easily have the same characteristics.) Nevertheless, in the case of the conscientious counselor who sees the injustice being done to students and begins a private campaign to get rid of the teacher, it will become counter productive. A private assessment with an administrator (who already knows about the teacher and has not been able to change or fire him/her) is valid. To make a public evaluation and campaign for purposes of removal can only breed conflict. Every teacher has his or her close friends in the school. The counselor who follows this approach will lose their support as well. To say it does not matter, is to fail to see that the loss of their cooperation will hurt students. Teacher evaluations and accountability are the prime responsibility of the teacher's administrator or supervisor. It is their responsibility to deal with the issues involved. For the counselor to get publicly involved can have adverse effects with **union members** as well.

Counselors Visiting Classrooms

Counselors wishing to visit classrooms for an **extended** amount of time should obtain clearance from the department chairperson and publish a calendar. If the counselor has to deliver an important impromptu message to a student, try to do it at the beginning or end of a class. The teacher will appreciate the fact that the counselor did not interrupt the lesson.

Compliment Teachers

Whenever the counselor gets the chance, compliment and thank faculty members for writing college recommendations or for their presence and contributions at meetings. If the counselor can do this in the presence of parents, or other significant people, it is even more appreciated. If not, a note from the counselor to his/her department head indicating the fine service rendered goes a long way to establishing positive relationships.

People under Pressure

One of the skills counselors should possess is the ability to recognize people under pressure. Whether they are students under stress, teachers feeling the pressure of their job, administrators, or fellow counselors who are wilting under the many tasks of their position, a proactive counselor should step in and try to ameliorate the problem. If nothing can be done, at least convey your sense of awareness and concern.

The Value of Chitchatting

The more counselors know the staff (their hobbies, sports interest, health, family, temperament, academic orientation, etc.) the greater the relationships, hence the greater the working compatibility. Naturally, it takes time and involvement to attain this goal, but the benefits to students are enormous. The approach is proactive. Many of these teachers feel comfortable coming to the counselor in the best interest of students. This approach does not advocate extended conversations. When the counselor gets the chance to make a contact, do so. One of the benefits of getting out of the office and standing in the hallway, etc. is that faculty will stop to chat.

Associating with Teachers

Any occasion to meet socially or share a common interest with teachers is vital for good relationships. It will enhance counselor effectiveness with students. Counselors, who isolate themselves at lunchtime from eating with the faculty, gain a reputation for being anti-social. Sometimes it is very difficult to get away at lunchtime to be in the faculty lunchroom, but an occasional visit goes a long way to building better working relationships with staff. Additionally, the counselor picks up a great deal of information on what is going on in school and the different personalities of teachers.

A Bad Reputation

It cannot be re-iterated how much the counselor needs teachers' help in aiding students. A counselor's poor reputation puts this necessity in jeopardy. A counselor who bad mouths teachers or is too lenient with students is definitely less effective.

Loss of Confidence

Counselors should never cover for a student. If so, counselors will then find themselves in a situation where they have a loss of confidence with staff. Then, counselor requests for help or advice will not be received with the same enthusiasm as that of a friend.

Senior Failures

No matter how long a guidance department has been in operation, there is always room for new procedures. If teachers give incompletes to seniors, a procedure must be in place where the counselor is quickly notified. Likewise, if a failure has been given to seniors late in the school year, both the teacher and the counselor must take action and the parent apprised of the consequences. In conjunction with the teacher, a plan for success should be worked out with the student and parent. Parents appreciate teacher and counselor phone calls that bring them up to date on a student's progress.

Students Kicked Out of Class

Occasionally, students are kicked out of class and told by the teacher to go to guidance and drop the course. Teachers are usually not permitted to do this. However, if the student is constantly disrupting the class and causing other students not to learn, then the teacher should confer with an administrator for approval to drop or change the student, not send the disruptive student to the guidance office to cause more trouble there. The counselor should work with the teacher on how to process the change. In this way, the counselor will not become a baby sitter and the teacher will appreciate the fact that the counselor helped solve the problem.

A Good Word

At meetings of a professional nature, when it is appropriate, mention the name of a teacher who has been most helpful. Word gets out that you are proactive in the teachers' behalf and willing to recognize a job well done. Another proactive sign is passing along to teachers, parents' positive comments. When parents make negative comments or will be taking action against a teacher, a heads up notice to the teacher is wise and appreciated.

Students in Danger of Failing

Report cards and progress reports of imminent student failures alert parents. However, there are times when these reports do not reach parents because of the interception or misdirection of the mail. Parents appreciate a call by the counselor with the notification of the failure or some other problem. A call is also a back up measure against the complaint: "How come I was never notified?" This is the teacher's primary responsibility but counselors who are knowledgeable of family problems can extend themselves. Phones are located in the teachers' phone room or the Guidance Office for teachers' convenience.

Remembering Names

Remembering the names of students, parents and teachers is an art. Some come by it naturally; others have to work at it. Nothing impresses a parent, student or teacher more than when the counselor calls them by their first name or proper last name. It is a sign of the counselor's interest in them. When a person is introduced to you, it is easy to be distracted by the issue at hand and the name will slip out of your mind. It takes a concentrated effort to pause and mentally repeat the name in your mind. Then try to associate the name with the person by some characteristic of their body, some event associated with the person, or an item associated with the name. It is a shame to hear students comment that the counselor could not even remember their name after four years. It is an art well worth cultivating.

A Question ?

Do you say hello to teachers, secretaries, custodial staff, hall monitors and cafeteria staff with the same enthusiasm and warmth as you give your favorite parent, administrator or student?

Give Details

When communicating with staff, it is good Public Relations to go into detail on the work the counselor has done relative to the discussion. Often times, staff does not realize the amount of work that goes into solving a problem. Counselors should not take for granted that staff members have an understanding of the work involved.

Ear to the Ground

Counselors are not always privy to information that coaches and teachers come by. A good relationship with staff members puts them at ease with the counselor and makes them far more willing to share information. Their input can be invaluable when counseling a student or parent and in making decisions that affect the student's plan for success.

A Guidance Manual for Counselors and Teachers

It is suggested that the guidance department create a "Manual for Counselors and Teachers." It should contain all procedures that relate to the guidance department and spell out each procedure for: guidance passes, test dates, parental conferences, teacher-counselor conferences, class visits, etc. This document saves a great deal of time and helps to assure that the proper procedures are followed. It should contain pertinent guidance documents: SAT test dates, guidance forms used through out the year, procedures for grade reporting, guidance pass procedures, etc. It is an excellent idea to share this document at the beginning of the school year with all staff members and is especially useful in the orientation of new staff. This handbook would contain information that even the most experienced teacher will find useful. It is naive to believe that staff knows everything about AP testing, how to write a college recommendation, the latest SAT/ ACT testing dates, guidance procedures, and much more. Excerpts from this handbook can easily be shaped into an orientation manual. Of special note in the manual is the need for **a good working relationship** between teachers and counselors.

Other People's Work

Counselors are so overloaded to begin with that they should not take on other people's work, as stated previously. Teachers, psychologists, social workers, students and administrators should be doing their own work and not passing it onto the counselor. Counselors should be helpful in the process but avoid becoming involved. Here is a sample list:

1. Looking up information which teachers have access

2. Allowing others: psychologists, administrators, students, teachers, etc. to pass work onto the counselor. Do not accept the directive, "Here is the report you requested. It is an original and you'll have to duplicate it and return it to me." Or, "I do not have time for this, you handle it." Politely, explain that as a matter of professional courtesy when the

counselor delivers reports to staff members it is their copy and they are not required to duplicate it and return it. Likewise, because a professional does not have time to follow up on something that is their responsibility, does not give them the right to pass it along to the counselor.

3. Do not allow department heads to impose on counselors parental notifications when they should be doing it. At times, a department will generate a list of students who have to be notified of a make up test, additional work, or a procedure to be followed. Simply to pass this on to the counselor is unfair. If it is to be done, the directive should come through the **guidance department chairperson** who knows school policies and is on guard to protect the counselors from invasive directives.

4. Do not make phone calls to parents that teachers should be making. If teachers direct the counselor to phone home regarding a student's poor performance, first ask if the teacher has been in contact. If yes, then make the call. If no, then be firm that the teacher makes the first contact.

5. There are rare occasions when even the guidance director is at fault in passing administrative work onto the counselors. A horizontal dialogue as described in the epilogue may be of some help here in solving the problem.

When in doubt, clarify the issue. Work with the guidance chairperson and get counsel on how to proceed to eliminate such practices. Be helpful but not inveigled into doing extra work. There is little enough time to get your own work done.

A School Community Effort

One of the major premises of this handbook is that guidance is a school community effort, each staff member working for the benefit and improvement of the student body. Cooperation is essential and the counselor needs everyone's help. Counselors, who think that they can accomplish what is best for students by themselves, are deceiving themselves. Counselors should never allow themselves to become passive in their effort to gain the cooperation of teachers. Teachers appreciate a counselor who can make firm decisions and affirm the truth. However, there are times when, in adversarial situations, a little bit of honey is better than bitter words. It is all a matter of developing the art of diplomacy so that good relations with staff members are maintained. This is a skill and has to be developed over time.

THE ART OF DIPLOMACY

There is an old Irish proverb which best defines this art:
Diplomacy is the ability
To tell a man to go to h_ _ _
So that he will look forward to the trip.
(Taken from the private "Collection of Irish Proverbs" by Eileen Taylor)

CHAPTER 9

Guidance and Public Relations

Note Achievements

This handbook is an effort to clarify the role of the counselor and to assist counselors in enhancing their image, both with the staff and parents. A book alone cannot do the job, but the consistent day-to-day professional application to the job will eventually win out. A technique recommended at the parent/student college planning session is to take special note of the students' achievements. If appropriate, take the opportunity as a school representative to tell the parents that the student is a credit to his/her parents and a real contributor to making the school a better place. "Your son/daughter is at the heart of what makes our school a great school." This may be the only time parents hear from a school official this commendation and it is appreciated.

Parent Calls

Counselor alert! On rare occasions when parents call to speak regarding their children, these parents may be excluded from contact by court order or the divorce contract. It is well to review those students who are so designated. If the counselor's computer carries the parental contacts, it is an easy way to check if the contact is allowed. Failure to do so can lead to embarrassing problems. If the computer does not supply this information, a list should be supplied to the counselor by the department head.

Dual Custody

Whenever possible, counselors should check to see if parents have dual custody and make sure they are on the mailing list for all reports, notifications, etc. Usually this is taken care of by the school registrar. When the information comes to the counselor's attention by way of a complaint, notify the registrar.

Bad News

If the counselor has to deliver a message to a parent regarding a failing student or one who may not be graduating, preface the remarks with the statement, "I'm calling because I am so concerned and must let you know…….." Demonstrate real interest and, if possible, a strategy to solve the problem while at the same time delivering the bad news. Do it in such a way that the parents will not say, "The only time we hear from the counselor, is when there is bad news."

Quick Chats

When leaving the building, if the counselor recognizes a parent in a car, he or she should have a quick chat with the parent to build up a good relationship. It need not be long. If the counselor is delayed, the counselor may suggest that he/she will be late for a meeting and must hurry on.

Indicate Your Efforts

The counselor, when dealing with parents on the phone, should not hesitate to indicate the lengths he/she has gone to solve a problem for their son or daughter. For the most part, parents do not understand the inner working of guidance services and it is well for their education that the counselor relays all the steps involved.

Our Side of the Story

It is important that counselors maintain a good reputation in the community. Unfortunately, students can twist and turn counselor statements. If this occurs, the counselor should contact all parties involved and explain exactly what happened. If necessary, call a conference to clarify the issue.

Know the Community

It is sad to relate that some young counselors do not receive tenure because they have no sense of the community, its culture, philosophy, and values. If a counselor is out of touch with community values, the counselor's treatment of students, though well intentioned, may be off the mark. A grasp of community values is attained through its academic concern for school improvement, from local papers, the amount of personal interest parents have in their children, frequency of parental contact with the counselor, dominant religious values, sports and social values. Conversations, especially with parents and fellow counselors and teachers will help to inform the new counselor.

Damage Control

When the counselor is wrong….he/she is wrong. Come up with a solution, minimize the damage, and move on quickly. The less said about it, the more quickly it is forgotten.

Case Study

A counselor was accused of not knowing one of his/her students by a parent. The counselor tried to explain that the young man was a good student and a freshman. He was not overlooked; he just did not need immediate service. At that time of the year, the counselor explained he was tied up with senior college applications. The young man had never actively sought out the counselor as well. Of course, this explanation did not satisfy the parent. The next day, however, the counselor did see the freshman and learned more about him, his interests and goals. Additionally, the counselor learned that the young man was an avid Yankee fan. It so happened that a few weeks later the counselor was given a Yankee calendar. The counselor remembered the student and, instead of giving the calendar directly to him, mailed it home. It was a sign to the parents of the counselor's interest and knowledge of the student. Gradually, a better relationship with the parent was restored. The astute counselor realized it would take time to restore parental confidence and found a way to rebuild it. In addition, as they say in New York, "You can't beat the Yankees!" …Just joking, all you out of town Yankee lovers.

Eaten Bread is Soon Forgotten

The expression, "Eaten bread is soon forgotten," is used again in this handbook when referring to students who take for granted the hard work the counselor does for them. Here it is used to emphasize, that in spite of the fact that many services are performed for parents, they will forget them as soon as the counselor makes a mistake. It is part of human nature and the counselor, because he/she is a professional, must get over it, and continue to do a good job for the parent and student.

"The man, who can make hard things easy, is the educator." Emerson (As recommended by Sam Stern, Esq.)

CHAPTER 10

Guidance, the Superintendent and
The Board of Education

"All Good Things Come from Above"

Perhaps this is the shortest chapter in the handbook, but one of the most important! It is from the top that the school community gets its spirit and financial backing. Fortunately, superintendents and board members are well informed when it comes to guidance services.

However, there are exceptions and a prime concern of counselors is the possibility that those in leadership roles have no real knowledge of the inner workings of the guidance department. Some members of the board have a peripheral knowledge based solely on their children's experiences. Some superintendents have not come up through the ranks and consequently know guidance from their point of view based on the services they need. Their understanding of guidance may be superficial and lack an in-depth understanding of the counselor's role and job description. There is apprehension among counselors that decisions will be made for economic reasons, which may influence the work of the counselor, and eventually may undermine the needs of students. It is the purpose of this handbook on guidance services to add to the Superintendent and Board's knowledge while contributing to their efforts to enhance school guidance programs. (Superintendents and Board members are invited to review **The Epilogue and Addendum 10** for approaches to evaluating and improving school guidance services for students.)

New Programs

Most schools experience growth through the initiation of new programs. In the course of putting these programs together, every aspect of the new program is considered: benefits to students, teacher training, financial cost, impact on teaching staff, etc. Unfortunately, some school administrators give little consideration to the impact these programs will have on counselors and how they will affect their services to students.

Case Study

An example of such an innovative program is the introduction of a new computer system, "E School" for scheduling and various registrar functions. A second example is the introduction of the International Baccalaureate Program. Both programs provided immense benefits to the school. Training for all the staff, including the counselors was required and generously afforded. However, there was only one consideration left out. What impact these programs would have on the counselor's workload? The E School program turned out to be very labor intensive, requiring a great deal of extra time on computer input. The IB program required additional counseling time. It was necessary to explain the program to students and parents and to determine if the student wanted to be a diploma or certificate candidate. Additionally, throughout the year, many schedule adjustments had to be made. Counselors have flexibility and can adjust. It is, nonetheless, unfair to hold them to the same accountability for all past areas of responsibility before these programs came along. Such programs as group counseling, dealing with "at risk students," college planning, CSE meetings, scheduling, etc. are all time consuming and are impacted by new programs. Complaints from counselors that they are "over loaded" originate out of such innovative programs that do not provide for assistance.

A good example of holding a rushed counselor accountable is when an egregious mistake in scheduling a special education student is made and a parent complains. Immediately all of his/her superiors are on his/her case. What is focused on is the outstanding mistake and not the fact his/her caseload has been impacted by new programs and no provision has been made for the loss of time to assure such mistakes are not made.

A Plea

One of the purposes of the many anecdotes and case studies in this handbook is to orchestrate the great work that counselors perform and the impact they have on students. What cannot be measured is the extent of their influence. Is it possible to answer the flowing questions?

How many are the number of students who have improved their conduct and academic performance through the advice of the counselor?

How many students have been encouraged to carry on despite personal family or in school social problems?

How many acts of despondency, including suicide, have been prevented?

How many acts of in-school violence have been nipped in the bud by a counselor's intervention?

How many students have been helped with peer conflicts, anger and grief management, and poor self-concepts, etc.?

Many of the student problems mentioned above are confidential and do not come to the attention of administrators. In the arduous task of budget planning when the board is under pressure to make cuts or add new duties to the counselor's case load, it is easy to forget the crucial services counselor provide.

Every problem a student has in his/her young life will eventually affect academic performance. Any help the counselor provides is a contribution to the **academic growth** of the school community. The plea to administrators and members of the board of education is **to realize the hidden values** in the counselor's work and provide the necessary time to deal with "students at risk."

The Guidance Time Pattern

On occasion, central administration will ask counselors for information to meet Board of Education demands. If possible, a reasonable amount of time should be given for the return of this information. As a courtesy to the counselor, knee jerk requests by the Board should be avoided. Such times as the opening of school in September, the college crunch in December, the scheduling for next year in February and March, and CSE meetings in the spring are times of great counselor pressure. Any consideration given to these times will be of great assistance to the counselor. If the information is needed during these times, affording the counselor a reasonable period of preparation is essential.

"Reason and calm judgment,
These qualities specifically, belong to a leader" Tacitus (As recommended by Latin Scholar, Dr. Sherman Payne)

CHAPTER 11

Guidance and Secretaries

Guidance Secretaries and Counselors

Unsung Partners

No one, more than the school guidance secretary, sets the tone for the guidance office! Secretaries' kindness and concern for students are as important as that of the counselor. The manner in which they greet students and respond to parents establishes a working relationship that can be either positive or negative. It is therefore essential for the guidance secretaries to reach out to students and parents in a caring way. Beyond their public relations skills, secretaries should be competent and informed. They are included in this handbook because their professionalism contributes to the overall good of the department.

It is extremely difficult to measure how much a counselor depends on the prudence, wisdom, and generosity of guidance secretaries. The correct and prudent information they give to students and parents facilitates the counselors' work. If there were a few words of caution for secretaries, they would be to make sure they have the facts and never to overreach their role as secretaries in giving advice.

Overwhelmed!

Counselors are so overwhelmed with paper work that they need to utilize their secretaries' help whenever possible:

1. Making out guidance passes
2. Screening phone calls
3. Prioritizing appointments
4. Clearing appointments with the counselor before scheduling them
5. Alphabetizing and filing
6. Making phone calls for the counselor
7. Reminding counselors of upcoming events
8. Supplying counselors with information
9. Preparing documents for distribution
10. Calming parents and students before seeing the counselor
11. Making reasonable excuses for the counselors when they are delayed for an appointment
12. Reminding counselors of important items to be followed-up
13. Covering for counselor mistakes
14. Spotting student evasive techniques to miss class
15. Calming teachers down
16. Managing the office
17. Typing documents
18. And on and on...

Overwhelmed Again!

Counselors are not the only ones overwhelmed in the guidance office. More often then not, the guidance secretaries are. They experience the same pressures as the counselor: processing college applications, generating guidance newsletters, dealing with multiple crises in the outer office, calming frustrated students waiting to see their counselor, dealing with rude students and parents, etc. At times, they are torn between the demands of the counselor and an administrator, each demanding a service. Since secretaries are the counselors' best allies, when counselors get the chance, they should reciprocate and help the secretaries out. A case in point is the stuffing of envelopes. Not that the counselor should stuff them, but going to a study hall and getting volunteers to help out is appreciated by the secretaries and the pay back is well worth the effort.

Reaching Students

Many times students fail to come for an appointment. It is then necessary to track them down. If the secretary has an aide or student volunteer, they are to be sent. Realizing that teachers do not like to have their class interrupted by messengers, it is best to send students at the beginning or end of the period.

When All Else Fails

In an effort to reach students, when all else fails, secretaries usually help by personally going to the classroom and getting the student for the counselor, especially if a sensitive issue is involved. If for some reason all other efforts to locate the student fail, the counselor should go and find the student. "Strike while the iron is hot," usually gets the job done and there is no need for a follow up.

At the End of the Day

At the end of the day, be sure to thank your secretaries for their day's work on your behalf. Never let secretaries feel that they are taken for granted. As the counselor leaves for the day, a departing thank you is a good habit. A consistent "Thank you" reinforces the counselor's sense of gratitude. It is well to note here, in many instances, counselors stay well beyond secretarial hours and the above suggestion may have to be implemented at another time.

Over Stepping Their Boundaries

When secretaries have been on the job for many years, they have learned a great deal about policy and procedures. It is up to the chairperson of the department to guide the secretaries as to what to tell the public. A well-informed secretary can, in good faith, be making decisions that alone belong to the counselor or department head.

Our Best Defense

An experienced secretary knows how to deal with the public. When the counselor is at a luncheon and a parent calls, the secretary could easily share the information, "He/she is not here right now and is attending a luncheon." This says it as it is, but the public may not see it as a well-deserved break, but rather as another perk that wastes the taxpayer's money and makes the counselor unavailable. A better response would be to indicate that the counselor is out of the building at a meeting and will return the call shortly.

Anecdote

The Wrong Answer

On one occasion, a parent entered a guidance office and inquired if the secretary could assist him. The secretary replied, "I'm not here right now. I'm on my break." She sat down, and continued, "Kindly wait until I come back." At least she said, "Kindly," but in no way did she indicate that she would help nor did she reflect an attitude that was supportive of guidance services. (As unlikely as this anecdote may seem, it actually happened to the author.)

> *"Self sacrifice is the real miracle*
> *out of which all the reported miracles grow."*
> Emerson (As suggested by Julia Eckley)

CHAPTER 12

Guidance, the Beginning
Counselor and the Intern

Nothing Can Replace Experience

For the beginning counselor or intern, guidance is one field that cannot be covered totally in a graduate classroom or a handbook such as this. Everyday in the school environment is a learning experience and no matter how long you are in the field, you will always be learning. I hope that this handbook will give you a jump-start. Throughout this handbook, the focal point has been the student but the handbook is also for the beginning guidance counselor and the intern. Every chapter in the handbook is applicable for the beginning counselor and the intern and will serve as a guide in times of uncertainty. In addition to reading this handbook, begin to read the school board policy handbook, state graduation regulations, and the school curriculum guide. These publications will fill you in on procedures and will save you from making many mistakes. Do it now while you are motivated, since these publications are a must and later on, you will be too busy.

The Curriculum Guide

New counselors should be thoroughly familiar with the curriculum guide (course description handbook.) Parents and students will be asking for course descriptions, pre-requisites, and level placement. Do not embarrass yourself by making a mistake. If in doubt, refer to the curriculum guide.

Case Study

Inadvertently, a counselor placed a student in Drawing and Painting I. The counselor failed to check if there was a pre-requisite, which there was, Studio Art I. After a few days, the teacher sent the student back to the counselor, indicating that the student was misplaced and needed a change in schedule. Unfortunately, for the counselor, before any adjustment could be made, the parent went to the principal and demanded that the counselor be written up for incompetence. In the world of mistakes, this is not earth shattering, but it is very embarrassing. Most of all, it reflected on the counselor's professionalism and reputation in the community.

Graduation Requirements

New counselors should memorize every aspect of their state's graduation requirements. No matter what the level of the school, know the transition requirements for the next level.

1. Know the exceptions (regulations for special education students, etc.)

2. Know alternate ways of meeting the state requirements.

3. Constantly review student transcripts for eligibility require-ments.

4. Keep a list of seniors and the requirements (courses) they may need to graduate.

Competency Tests

In some states, if students do not meet a level of proficiency in certain subject areas, they may be required to take competency exams. In some cases, this applies to students who are classified. Whatever the regulations, a special list of these students has to be maintained. Who is responsible for checking this list? Whether it is a department head or the director of special education, the counselor should keep his/her own list. It is suggested that the list be divided into columns listing:

1. The names of all the students who need to take competency tests
2. The subject area
3. The students who have passed the test
4. The students who need to pass the test
5. In what cohort does the student belong? (The cohort is the year in which the student began the ninth grade.) This may determine the number of tests to be taken.

The requirements from year to year may differ and it is the cohort to which the individual student belongs that will determine the tests to be taken. The counselor's list should be checked against the official list maintained by the supervising department head.

Why Me?

The new counselor may say, "Why should I be doing all kinds of checking when other people are responsible for it? The answer is twofold:

1. They are your students and their welfare should be your concern. Keeping up on their requirements helps you guide and motivate them.
2. No matter who is responsible for a mistake, somehow or other, the counselor is always dragged in on the problem. Let us face it; no one likes **to go down alone.**

Extra Help

In instances where a student has failed a required subject or competency exam that is required for graduation, the district is usually responsible for providing extra help for these students. A periodic check to see if the students are attending these extra help sessions should be made by the person in charge. If they are not attending, a notification to the parents should be sent home. The counselor can assist by doing his/her own check, especially for students who are in serious jeopardy of not graduating.

Professionally Responsible

Interns should be aware of situations they find themselves where they will be held professionally responsible.

Case Study

There may be an occasion when an intern is asked by a parent or teacher to work with a student who has emotional problems. This is a wonderful compliment. However, if the student became unruly, began to throw things, and injured himself or another student, the intern and the school would be held liable. The intern does not have the training or experience (or certification) to deal with this kind of student. The intern should immediately confer with his advisor or department head before taking on such a student. Better yet, the intern should immediately deny the request. He should have been trained to avoid such a possibility from the start.

Guidance Interns Interviewing for Jobs.

Every guidance intern will have to interview to get a counseling job. There are many approaches to interviewing for a job. In the counseling field, the importance of demonstrating real concern for students and the manner in which the intern will reach out to them are paramount. (Addendum 2) The interviewing committee is not only looking for professional competency but for genuine concern and interest in students.

Failure to demonstrate this concern by tone, bodily enthusiasm and personal commitment is a fundamental interviewing mistake.

College Recommendations and Letter Writing Skills

Interns should take the opportunity to review the college recommendations of senior counselors and practice writing recommendations of their own. The same applies to letter writing and reports. This may constitute a major component of a counselor's work. Job screening interviews will require a written sample of the prospective counselor's writing skills. (See Chapter 19, College Recommendations for more ideas.)

Go Slowly

If the opportunity is given an intern to become a counselor, do not take on too many extra responsibilities. Better to do a good job with what you are supposed to do than to be overwhelmed by too many extra volunteer jobs. The new counselor's main responsibility is to students, getting to know them and being available to see them. Beginning counselors will be judged not on the wonderful extra-curricular things they have accomplished, but on the competency and professionalism they bring to counseling.

Save Your Opinions.....

Save your opinions until they are asked for. In the beginning, new counselors should be conservative in making recommendations for change or advocating new programs. Better to get to know the lay of the land before becoming innovative. The beginning counselor may not know whose feet he/she might be stepping on. Go with the flow until well established and more experienced in school politics before beginning new programs or procedures. Be a team player and do your job well...then give your opinions. They will be more respected.

When to Take on an Extra Curricular Activity

Once the new counselor is established and feels comfortable in the position, take on an activity that is not too time consuming. Such activities as an International club, a Partners club, SADD, etc. are community minded and help the counselor build strong relationships with students. The students in these clubs are usually very generous and will reach out to other students. They will become the core of the helpers the counselor will need to do volunteer work and to implement other projects the counselor may wish to initiate.

Anecdote

Throughout the handbook are suggestions to help students to assimilate into the school community. Such clubs as an International club, Partners, etc. can be a great asset to counselors in this area. Suggested activities are: "A Welcoming Ceremony for New Students," an evening event for ELL parents, posting inspirational sayings throughout the building, assisting in a recognition ceremony for students who are at risk and who are making an effort to pass academically. These are all related counselor activities and can easily become part of a club's agenda. One word of caution is the sensitivity the counselor has to employ in using students to perform certain aspects of each event.

Get Your Own Volunteer Workers

A wonderful opportunity is offered the beginning counselor when counseling students. If you have intelligent students who are looking to build up the volunteer aspect of their resume, enlist them on the spot to become one of your workers. This is especially opportune if they have a free period in their schedule and can come to the counselor on a regular basis. Such jobs as filing, getting students, compiling surveys, acting as a tutor, helping the secretaries, etc. are invaluable time savers.

Needy Students as Volunteers

In every school, there are needy students who need someone to take an interest in them. They may not be the brightest, nor the most responsible, and require constant supervision and encouragement. If the counselor offers these students the opportunity to work in the guidance office, it is a real confidence builder. However, these students usually demand a great deal of attention and follow up. Counselors should only take on this task if they are experienced and can handle this type of student without interfering with their regular duties.

Peer Counseling

Peer counseling utilizes the respect students have for one another, especially underclassmen for seniors. It is a great tool but must be undertaken with the counselor present. The counselor's presence assures that no peer counselor may inadvertently give bad advice. Peer counselors should be trained well in advance of the first meeting. Once again, the students who are part of the counselor's club or volunteers from his/her counseling caseload make excellent peer candidates.

The advantages of peer counseling:
1. Needy students are helped and motivated.
2. There is bonding with the needy students and their peer counselors.
3. The influence and friendship of the peer counselors extend beyond the setting of the group into the classroom, the ball field, and social activities.
4. There is identification with the counselor.
5. Students on the counselor's caseload gain added activities for their resume.
6. Word gets out of the good work being done by the group and the counselor.

Beginning Counselors and Tenure

It is the aspiration of all beginning counselors that some day they will receive tenure.

Here are a few pointers that may help in the process.

1. Deadlines...meet them!

2. Make sure your reports are accurate and complete.

3. Be on time for meetings and be prepared.

4. Review transcripts for accuracy and completeness, at least twice a year.

5. Be kind to students.

6. Follow up requests from administrators, parents, and teachers.... immediately

7. Be visible!

8. Be involved in departmental activities.

9. Be a team player.

10. Do not leave on time for at least the first three months

11. Establish a reputation for being generous with your time.

12. Know your school's community culture.

13. **Be nurturing to students.**

14. **Etc.**

"Trust yourself and you will know how to live." Goethe
(As used in the novel **"Hour of the Cat"** by Peter Quinn)

PART TWO

THE MECHANICS
OF
GUIDANCE

CHAPTER 13

Motivation

"A Picture Is Worth......"

Whenever the counselor can, ask students for pictures that relate to their special talents and place them on the bulletin board. This technique shows your interest and the student is usually very pleased to be so highly regarded. It is amazing how proud students are to have their work or picture displayed. It is also significant how many other people who come into the counselor's office will relate to such pictures, especially parents.

Anecdote

When being admitted, a student from South America spotted a memento brought back from Peru for the counselor by one of his counselees. It immediately put the youngster at ease. It gave her assurance that there were other Peruvians in the school to befriend and her non-English speaking parents were elated as well.

Use the Public Address System to Motivate Students.

An easy strategy to implement is the use of the public address system to share an inspirational idea or quote. There are many books of inspirational sayings that are suitable for the daily announcement. Purchase one and check off the quotes you want read. Show the book to the principal and clear the idea of a daily quote to inspire students. Then, request whoever types up the daily announcements to place a quote in the bulletin each day. Once this is done, it is smooth sailing until you run out of quotes. In a school of hundreds where each student has his/her own personal problems, the daily quote will surely have an impact.

A similar motivational technique is to place banners with significant quotes throughout the school. The use of volunteers to do this is essential. The job of the counselor is to supply the quotes and let the volunteers do the rest.

Middle School Students

When the senior high school counselor has the opportunity, it is well advised to visit the middle school seventh and eighth grade students to discuss the college admissions process.

While this may seem a bit of a reach, nonetheless, these students must be presented a reason for applying themselves and improving their academic performance in middle school. Their present grades will not become part of their permanent high school transcript (no need to mention this), unless the student is in specialized courses that carry high school credit. However, middle school students must be taught to realize that the academic skills they develop and the athletic, cultural, and volunteer activities they are perfecting will contribute to their college acceptance. **(See Addendum 12.)**

Another motivating technique is to use seniors, who are about to go on to college and have come up through the system, to speak to middle school students. Their experiences, good and bad, can be shared. Naturally, the senior students who are chosen for this motivational project must be mature, diversified, and carefully screened.

High School Students

Two similar seminars may be conducted with tenth graders or even ninth graders. One is to have a college admissions counselors relate what colleges are looking for in a student. (College reps can become accustomed or even bored with visiting schools. A change of pace is appreciated and it becomes a memorable experience. It will be memorable in the sense that the high school will standout in their memory when they read applications from that school.) The other technique is to use college freshman who will relate their experiences. This group must be well screened and each alumni given a specific topic to avoid repetition.

For Seniors

For seniors headed off to college, a similar college alumni group can be part of an overall program to advise seniors on practical matters in their transition. A workable program may consist of a panel of alumni and guidance counselors. Each counselor can introduce a specific topic with a brief refection of his /her own and then introduce the screened alumni to respond to the same question. This procedure prevents alumni, who love to scandalize, from relating bizarre college behaviors.

The Principal as Motivator

In every school, students see the principal as the ultimate authority figure. Principals are respected by students for their power, their wisdom, and the role they play in their lives. Why not take advantage of this position to motivate students? Without consuming much time, there are many instances where students can be brought to the principal's office to be recognized for their individual achievements. This presumes the counselor has a good working relationship with the principal and that the principal will make him/herself available for brief meetings, usually immediately after the announcements are read. Most principals enjoy these brief encounters with students and see the meetings as a means of keeping in contact with students.

If the Principal is Amenable

When a student achieves something significant such as "Student of the Month" at BOCES (an out of home school vocational center), take the student to the principal's office for a brief "hand shake." In addition to encouraging these students, it is a means of making them feel part of the home school. This procedure should be part of an understanding with the principal as indicated above.

Power Move

At the beginning of the year, an understanding should be established with the principal on how to deal with normally good students who are beginning to fall apart. When a student is performing poorly, failing to do homework, or handing in assignments late, and is generally falling apart academically, a meeting may be set up with the principal, student, and counselor. This should not be an everyday occurrence but reserved for students who are usually good students but suddenly have lost interest in their schoolwork and need a boost. It is understood that all other avenues of motivation have been tried before going to the principal.

Use the Principal's Office for Good Effect, Again

When the counselor perceives that a student who is falling apart academically requires an intervention, another good technique is to call the student to the counselor's office. The counselor then apprizes the student that he/she has been asked to set up a meeting in the principal's office to discuss the reason for the student's failing performance. (No real appointment is made at this time.) The student is informed that the principal's meeting can be canceled if improvement is demonstrated before the date of the meeting. If the student fails to improve, the counselor meets with the student at the appointed time. The counselor then indicates that the principal is unavailable, which is the case. Then, a real appointment is set up with the principal to discuss the student's behavior. This puts additional pressure on the student since the student, having gone through the process, will have second thoughts about the meeting with the principal. If all else fails, have the meeting.

Recognition Ceremony

In every school, there are multiple ceremonies to recognize outstanding academic and athletic students. Few, if any schools, have ceremonies to recognize those who are trying just to improve from failing to passing students. (Please refer back to **Chapter 4, Guidance and Administrators,** Using the Principal's Office for Good Effect regarding Steps in Organizing a Recognition Ceremony for Striving Students.

Always Tell the Truth

Whenever a student asks for advice or information on his transcript, always tell the truth. However, there are times if the information is not sought, it need not be given, especially if it will be beneficial for the student.

Anecdote

A junior came to his counselor to program his schedule for his senior year. His main request was that he takes as few courses as possible. He knew the requirements for graduation, which included three years of math. He asked that the counselor be sure to schedule him for the next level of math so that he could graduate. The counselor obliged, knowing full well that the student had met his math requirement by completing his occupational training course in auto mechanics. Inherent in the auto curriculum was a credit for math. When the student left, the counselor phoned his parents telling of his plan for their son. First, the student was to be a business major and an extra credit in math would be to his advantage. Secondly, the student was the bane of the assistant principal's existence, constantly disruptive in the hallways and a general nuisance. It would serve the student and the school well if he were in class learning, rather than roaming the halls. The parents were on board with this plan.

Since the student believed he needed the math course for graduation, he made a sincere effort to learn. At the end of the year, his parents told him of the service the counselor had performed in his behalf. Initially he was irate. However, after the graduation ceremony, he approached the counselor with the words, "You con artist, you put one over on me. I know it was for my good. I learned more math and was in less trouble." He then proceeded to give the counselor a good-natured hug.

Contacts

In the beginning of the school year, before the sixth grade or freshman orientation sessions, send each of your new students a note introducing yourself and telling them that as their counselor, you are there to help them. (Student volunteers can help here.) Sometimes, it is difficult to meet every new student at the beginning of the year and this note serves as an icebreaker. If the counselor is comfortable with this suggestion, have your picture photo copied on the message. In this way, students are able to recognize the counselor. Invite them to say hello to you whenever and wherever they see you. Productive relationships begin with mutual recognition and concern. (Sometimes these notes end up going home to parents, which is good P.R.)

Creating Student Rapport

Every time a student comes into the counselor's office take time for small talk and pleasantries. If you are all business, no real relationship is developed. This can be difficult when things are hectic, but even a few kind words will do the trick.

"Always Leave Them Laughing"

This paragraph could easily be called, "The Doctor's Bedside Manner," which is to say, "The Counselor's Desk Side Manner." A student's visit to the counselor's office is purposeful. This is not to say that the student is automatically at ease or comfortable. It is at these times when an icebreaker, which is cheerful and calming, can set the right tone for the meeting. At the conclusion of the meeting, just before the student leaves, the counselor should make some parting remark of a happy or comical nature that will become a reminder to the student that the counselor is a nice person to visit. It is also a good time to restate your concern for the student and to remind the student that he/she is always welcome. Some counselors may feel that stating their concern is stating the obvious. Students appreciate the fact that they are cared for and need the support this message gives. In addition, it is a message that will get out to other students.

Anecdote

Recently, on visiting a medical doctor's office, the patient heard the doctor's parting words, "Lov Ya!" This would not be especially appropriate for a counselor, but the concern and affection expressed aught to be captured by the counselor and related to the student in some way. Not every counselor will feel comfortable with the above style. Whatever technique the counselor uses, say something to bring the student back.

Enhancing a Student's Self Concept

When the counselor finishes the college recommendation for a student, it is good practice to read it to the student. The counselor's positive comments encourage the student in the college application process because it is always uplifting to hear something positive said about ones self. In addition, the student may suggest something the counselor has left out of the recommendation.

Detention Room

Whenever possible, the counselor should stop at the Detention Room. Check to see which students are yours. Take the time quietly to speak to these students for a few minutes to see why they are there and to encourage them. You will learn their behavior patterns and will be better able to counsel them in the future.

Case Study

There are times as the year comes to the end, seniors who are sure they will graduate, may disrespect a specific teacher. Such an incident occurred when a student threw a textbook into the garbage can and insulted the teacher. The counselor was called to intercede and find a solution that would satisfy the teacher and would enable the student to attend the graduation ceremony. First, the student had to apologize and made to realize that what was done was wrong in and of itself. He should apologize not just for the sake of attending the graduation ceremony but because it was the respectful and correct thing to do. Of course, academically graduation was in place since he had met all graduation requirements. Students generally cannot be denied a diploma over school disciplinary incidents. A student may be punished and derived of certain graduation privileges, but his diploma cannot be denied.

As a solution, the counselor contacted the student's parents and mapped out a strategy wherein the student would apologize and graduate with his class. With their approval and knowledge of the plan, the parents were to tell the student that he could not go to graduation practice and must see the counselor first. At this point, the senior associated the possibility of missing graduation practice with not getting a diploma and missing the graduating exercise. Plans of this nature are best implemented over the weekend when the student has time to sweat things out. Usually, by the time the student meets with the counselor, the groundwork is prepared for an apology. The student did come contrite to the counselor and the counselor suggested that in addition to an apology to the teacher, a bouquet of flowers should be given as a mark of good will. The strategy worked and the teacher was grateful for the apology and the flowers. The student learned a lesson and the parents enjoyed the graduation ceremony.

Use Progress Reports to Motivate

If a student is doing poorly in school, but indicates to the counselor a real desire to improve, a worthwhile technique is to have the student agree to bring weekly progress reports to teachers. When returned to the counselor, they are to be read just by the student and the counselor. They are not for the parents' eyes. Allow the week to pass and then see if the student has shown improvement. This is done with the understanding that they will not be sent home. If the reports are good, the student may even ask they be sent home. It is a means of verifying that the student is trying to do better. If the results are negative, they should be reviewed with the student. After the student leaves, they should be filed in the student's folder. (Should the counselor be accused of not helping the student, they are a proof of a valid attempt.)

During this same meeting, it should be agreed that another set of progress reports would be sent out in a week's time. It is with the student's understanding that if the results of the second progress reports are negative, they **will be sent home.** (An additional benefit of this procedure is that parents will receive unsolicited progress reports, again indicating that the counselor has been working with the student.)

Don't Beat a Dead Horse

Progress reports are a useful tool, if used properly. However, there are instances when parents want reports almost on a daily basis. This can be a case of over kill. If the first few reports from teachers have no effect and the parents cannot motivate their son or daughter, another means should be investigated. The same holds true for parent-teacher conferences. Too frequent use of this procedure only hardens the student who is subjected to a weekly or bi-weekly barrage of teacher negative comments. **Frequent subjection to negative comments only demoralizes students.** Approaches that are creative are needed. The student who is completely turned off and does not respond to progress reports or parent-teacher conferences, must be given a reason to achieve other than a continuous listing of failures. A better approach would be to have a teacher-parent conference, on techniques to motivate the student, without the student present. Creative approaches that enlist the interests and self-concept of the student should be discussed. A more personal approach on the part of the counselor and teachers is always a good first beginning in changing behavior.

Of special note to counselors and teachers is the fact that some parents hold them accountable for supplying inordinate amounts of information. There comes a point when counselors and teachers should take a stand (with the department head's approval). The information has already been supplied and more reports only continue to demoralize the student. Regular grade reporting and interim progress reports are already built into the system. Some other approach has to be suggested.

Case Study

There was the case of a young man who as a freshman was disruptive in class, disrespectful to teachers and constantly did not do his homework. On many occasions, he was sent in a fit of anger and despair to the guidance counselor. The only way to calm him down was to distract him with his interest in lacrosse. But even this interest was taken away from him when he could not get along with the coach. Naturally, all kinds of meetings, detentions, suspensions, and counseling sessions took place. Nothing seemed to work and by the time he was entering what should have been his junior year, it was one failing year after another. His parents would not grant his request to drop out of school. All other methods of motivation had failed. **It was time for some kind of creative solution.** His counselor had in mind an alternate school program, which only serviced classified students. First, the counselor recommended that the parents request from the CSE that their son be classified. In his case, he would be classified as emotionally impaired. Initially, when this suggestion was made, the parents were against it. However, the counselor explained that this program was specifically funded for such youngsters so that they can earn their GED and be given a job. Usually students cannot begin a GED program in their junior year. In this program, the student would receive counseling and support and could earn a GED. It was the right program and met the student's particular needs. The parents agreed. The next step was to have the Committee on Special Education approve his classification, which they did since his history gave sufficient evidence. The young man began the program, was under less pressure, less confinement, less regulations and he was making money at the same time. He was much happier about himself and consequently, he wanted to succeed.

Report to Colleges

When dealing with seniors who are doing poorly but are looking forward to college, remind them that academic reports at midyear will be sent to colleges. For many seniors, the mid year report is a determining factor in the college acceptance process and may help to motivate them throughout the year. Another technique is to have visiting admissions personnel speak individually to students who may be interested in their college but are doing poorly.

Accepted/Rejected

For those students admitted to college, the guidance department is obliged to send a final transcript to each student's prospective college. Rarely do colleges reject students once they are accepted. However, it does happen in those cases where seniors throw the anchor away and proceed to do miserably at the end of their senior year. More often, students who do poorly after being accepted are sent warning notices or put on probationary acceptance. Counselors are advised to collect a set of these notices and share them with such seniors.

Tips on Convincing a Student to Stay in a Course

When students come to the counselor requesting to drop a good course and the counselor disagrees, first discuss the ramifications of the change:

1. The impact on the schedule
2. The effect on the transcript for college acceptance
3. The alternate course required
4. The school policy on course changes
This procedure may influence the student's decision.

Bad News

Do not fall victim to being the bearer of bad news. If you have to assume this role, do it in a way that will not ruin your relationship with your students. For example, if a student has to double up in P.E. or take a required course, the counselor must place the student. However, try to lead the student to ask for the placement rather than simply imposing the placement. When the counselor allows the student to make this decision, it also empowers the student and may motivate him/her to do well in the course.

Faith in Students

Counselors deal with students who sometimes seem **hopeless** both academically and socially. The counselor's kindness and interest in such students may have no immediate effect, but down the road, people change and your **hope** and faith in them will be justified, remembered and appreciated.

Anecdote

A young man who struggled in school, dropped out and years later was in a severe automobile accident He returned to the counselor for her help and advice. She asked of the young man why he specifically came back to her for advice. He answered that, "I never forgot your kindness and, besides, don't you realize that I love you for it."

Mileage

Whenever the counselor is doing something favorable for a student, get the most mileage out of it. For example, the counselor makes a schedule change that a student wants. First, review the motivation for the change. Then say that you are in favor of the change but would want some proof or guarantee that the change will be productive. The student should give the counselor a plan, which could include a report, improved conduct in class, or a higher grade, **then** make the change. Simply to agree to a change without getting something productive from the student is a lost opportunity.

Non-Directive Counseling

The art of non-directive counseling is the ability to transfer information and advice in a manner that the student receives it without the feeling of being preached to or directed to change. Often times the counselor is made aware of a situation from a parent or a fellow student and asked to do something about it without giving the slightest indication that the counselor is privied to the situation. Such incidents as family sickness, personal problems of the student or conflict among peers, are cases in which the non-directive approach may be used effectively.

Anecdotes

If a parent reveals that a student is very anxious about flying and has to take a family trip, the parents may ask the counselor's help without revealing the source. In a case such as this, knowledge of the student's interests is valuable. If the young man is interested in sports, the counselor can direct the conversation to a sport such as football. Whatever the student's favorite team is, the counselor may pick an opposing team that has to travel in order to play a game. The counselor can then banter with the student about which is the better team. When it comes to the game, the counselor can then lead into how much certain players dislike flying in order to get to the game. (In football, John Madden won't fly.) Build on the interest of the student, who may or may not express his fears. At the appropriate moment, the counselor can then tell what techniques players use to allay their fear of flying. This technique is an art and a level of skill and sensitivity is required to carry it off.

Another technique employed to remind students of their obligations without embarrassing them in front of their peers, is to use "a misdirected request." As the counselor stands in his/her accustomed spot in the hallway and two students pass by, one of which is failing to do homework, the counselor can misdirect his advice by asking, in a jocose manner that the recalcitrant student to be in charge of making sure the good student is prepared for the class. The directive gets the recalcitrant student's attention, who regards it as a form of banter. He is reminded, without being embarrassed of his school issues and enjoys the approach.

Empowering Students

Developing good personal, counselor relationships with students is not easy! Some students are defensive, others shy and still others lacking in communication skills. However, a useful technique to overcome a social barrier is the use of a little reverse psychology. How can the student help the counselor? The trick to this technique is to find some skill, interest, or hobby the student has and the counselor lacks or wants to develop. If the student is engaged in explaining the skill, etc., he/she feels more at ease with the counselor. Better yet, if the counselor asks advice on how to develop this skill, the student becomes empowered. In so doing, social barriers begin to fade away. Such interests as fishing, mountain climbing, beauty hints, fashion designing, cooking, etc. can be utilized as a skill to be acquired. If the student helps the counselor acquire this skill over a period of time, the student identifies more with the counselor.

Anecdote

Fiddler Crabs

(Fiddler crabs are about a half inch in diameter and live among the rocks, crawling at a fast pace to search for food. They give a little sting with their claws if not handled properly. They are a delicious catch for black fish, which have blunt teeth designed by nature to crush the fiddler crab. They make good bait.)

Knowing a student's interest is helpful in many ways. During the course of a conversation, a young man spoke of his interest in fishing, especially at a seaside town a hundred miles away. It so happened that the counselor had a home there. So the counselor planned to go fishing with the student for black fish. The student was to get the bait, fiddler crabs, and the counselor would bring lunch. They did get some fish but many of the big ones got away.

The following week, back at school, an urgent request from the principal was made to the counselor, seeking his expertise and help to quell the hysterical screaming of many young women in the girls' bathroom. Someone had released **dozens of fiddler crabs** while the girls were using the facility.

The principal was in awe when the counselor came up with the culprit. She was to take punitive action and the counselor was to advise the individual. (Notice how both roles were clarified and the counselor was to act only as an adviser.)

This is one fish didn't get away. The first order of business was to discuss the ramifications of the young man's act. When suitably addressed as to the consequences of such a blatant act and his lack of prudence, the counselor had one final question to ask the student. Since they were fishing together only a week ago, he inquired good-naturedly: *Please explain to me the meaning of the phrase,* "Just how dumb can you be?" In the end, the relationship with the student was deepened, each sharing in a common "fiddler crab" experience.

Review Exactly What Is on a Transcript

Another good motivational technique, especially in the earlier high school grades is to go over exactly what is placed on a transcript. Explain that only final grades are placed at the end of each year. For the poor performing students, it gives them **hope** that they can change their grades before they become final. SAT and ACT scores are usually placed on the transcript: so are AP results. Mention that the higher the level of the courses, the more impressive is the transcript. There is also value in graphing the trends in the transcript on the blackboard, descending, ascending or consistent grades year after year. Mention how admission counselors can read these trends. This technique is valuable at a freshman orientation or for sophomores in a group counseling session.

Admission Personnel

Early on in a student's high school education, the concept that college admissions personnel are professionals should be ingrained in students. They are experts on reading transcripts, evaluating college essays and assessing student involvement. Nothing escapes them. If students understand this, it may help to motivate some of them. Such techniques as reviewing a college profile or requesting an admissions counselor to speak on "the evaluation of transcripts in the college acceptance process" will help students to understand that they are dealing with professionals who will not be deceived. At the better colleges, where they may have over 20,000 applications, they may be looking more to reject candidates than accept them at the final stages of the selection process.

Praise the Student to the Parent

Take every opportunity when the occasion legitimately arises to tell parents what a great kid they have. As counselors, we do not always know what is going on at home (sickness, family conflict, financial difficulties, etc.). When parents can get a bit of good news from the counselor, it means so much to them. Parental feedback to the student is a positive motivational force as well.

"We are what we repeatedly do.
Excellence, then, is not an act, but a habit." Aristotle
(As attributed to Lisa Donna)

CHAPTER 14

Confidentiality

The Educational Record

In educational law what is regarded as a student's **educational record** has many shaded areas. No matter how familiar the counselor is with the law, when in doubt go through the proper channels seeking advice from the school attorney. If there is any disagreement with any aspect of this chapter on "Confidentiality," the same advice applies. An explanation of confidentiality as regards the student's educational record, is provided by FERPA, the Family Educational and Privacy Act, and is found in **Addendum 8**. It is well worth the read. A case in point is when a student transfers into your district from a mental health institution, make sure that a psychological release from the institution and permission to attend school are included in the admission's admit packet. Students with psychological problems may wish to keep the information secret. However, the name of the sending institution is a tip off. For the good of the student body and teaching staff, if no transcript and permission to enter a regular high school come from a mental health facility, a follow up is absolutely necessary. When students transfer, the receiving school has the right for the complete "educational record" and does not need parental permission to request it.(FERPA)

Confidentiality

All information of a confidential nature should be safe guarded. It should be kept in a secure and locked place in the guidance office, assistant principal's office, psychologist's office, etc. Leaving doors open and cabinets unlocked invite trouble.

Counselor Anecdotal Records

The personal notes of the counselor may not have to be handed over to the courts if they do not become part of the student's "educational record." If they are meant less as an educational record but more as notes for the counselor's personal use to refresh his/her memory and if they are not shared, they may remain confidential. On the other hand, if they are used at a CSE meeting, a Child Study Team meeting or other meetings, they are considered as part of the student's educational record. An "educational record" may be defined as any folder wherein any educational information that pertains to the student is kept. This includes much more than the "cumulative folder." It extends to the assistant principal's records, the nurse's records, the attendance records, anywhere there is an "educational record" of the student.

Student-Counselor Confidentiality

In matters of health and safety, as in cases of abortion, self-abuse (cutting), suicidal ideation, etc., the counselor is obliged to notify the parents. In school, the counselor is acting in "loco parentis" and must act accordingly. In cases of drug and alcohol use, these are gray areas but once they affect the health and safety of the child, action must be taken. In such instances when the student is about to confide something of a confidential nature to the counselor, a warning to the student may be in order. If the information about to be told relates to the health and safety of the student or others, it will not be regarded as confidential.

Release of Information

Items such as rank in class, what percentile a student is in, any IEP and psychological information can only be disclosed with permission from the parent or if so ordered by the courts. Directory information, according to FERPA, can be disclosed, "without consent, such as a student's name, address, telephone number, date of and place of birth, honors and awards, and dates of attendance. However, schools must tell parents and eligible students about directory information and allow parents and eligible students a reasonable amount of time to request that the school not disclose directory information about them." FERPA

Subpoenas

Should a counselor receive a subpoena for the "educational records" of a student, the first step in the process is to notify the principal so that he/she can review the document.

Destroy Records

The counselor should destroy (shred) personal folders or records of any kind when they are about to be thrown out. At times, transcripts, minutes of meetings and other confidential information can be found in the trash basket, available for the reading.

Anecdote

A counselor, before interviewing for a position, took the opportunity to walk through the building after school and just observe. When she passed the guidance office and glanced in the trashcan, which was ready for disposal, she recovered a discarded transcript. At the interview, she mentioned this. Along with her other good qualities and her keen observation skills, she got the job. From that point on, all official documents and records had to be shredded.

Students and Confidential Files

Whenever student volunteers do filing, always be in their presence. Never allow students to work on confidential filing. Never allow them to work on the counselor's computer, even if the student does not enter confidential files, access to other sources of information is available.

Be Aware

If the counselor has the tendency toward self-aggrandizement, he/she should be careful not to reveal little bits of confidential information to shock or impress peers. Information is a great source of power to impress people.

Anecdotes

The teachers' cafeteria is a great place to pick up all kinds of information. Some teachers and counselors vie to be the most informed and the most in touch with their students. Information concerning confidential after school happenings, parental discussions and private student discussions are a great source of self-empowerment. Counselors are no exception to this rule. For some it is an outlet to justify that they are both working hard and impacting the lives of their students. Innuendos indicating that they are aware of certain confidential events and know more about the situation are a form of sharing information. The mere indication of confidential knowledge beyond what others have access to is a form of speculation that can boarder on disclosure.

Even more scandalous is information that is regarded as confidential at a PPS meeting, CSE meeting or a principal's meeting, etc., which is leaked by one of the "professionals" who attends such meetings. Some "professionals" thrive on sharing with their friends insider information on current teacher problems or other confidential bits of "juicy" information. Once information is leaked, it is not only a breach of ethics but jeopardizes open discussion at future meetings.

Misconception

It is a misconception to believe that the law protects all matters of a confidential nature that take place in the guidance office. On the contrary, the courts may request information shared in the guidance counselor's sessions. The confidentiality that the counselor has is not as absolute as that of a doctor or lawyer.

"Give everyone your ear, but few thy voice." Shakespeare
(As recommended by Shakespearian Scholar, Dr. Jerome Brennan)

CHAPTER 15

Tips for Beginning Counselors
And Interns

"Learn the Ropes"

It is difficult to group all the diverse areas of information that the beginning counselor has to deal with into one handbook. Consequently, when giving tips to the beginning counselor and intern, some exemption must be made if not all areas are covered. The best advice for the young counselor is to seek the wisdom and experience of your peers. **Chapter 5** speaks of the necessity for counselors to relate to teachers. However, it is even more important that the young counselor makes a determined effort to relate to fellow counselors. Their help goes beyond advice. The main issue is that the beginning counselor and intern should "learn the ropes." There are two ways of doing this. The first is to be "knocked to the canvas" by your mistakes. The second is to learn "to bounce off the ropes" by listening to your "coaches."

Do not Forget the Prerequisites

Each year, schools issue a Student Course Selection Booklet. From year to year, course descriptions and prerequisites may change. If the counselor fails to remember the prerequisites and places a student in a course inappropriately, be prepared for an on-rush of teachers, administrators and parents to address the error.

The teacher is incensed that you wrongly placed a student in their exclusive course.

The administrator is upset that you might be overloading the course.

The parent is furious that now the student has to go about rearranging his/her schedule.

It is well to read the Course Selection Book each year and highlight significant or even minor changes.

Anecdotes

On an incoming transcript, the mistake of missing a course taken in the eighth grade that is generally not offered can cause a major problem. A case in point is that Environmental Studies is generally not offered in the eighth grade for high school credit. The counselor missed it on the transcript and two years later rescheduled the student for Environmental Studies. The parent was so furious that his child was repeating a subject, he demanded that the counselor be changed and maneuvered to have the title of the course also changed. In this way, the student would receive a course credit for the eight-grade course and the repeated course. The counselor was not advised of this problem until after all the changes were made. Both the principal and the parent were satisfied with this solution. Ironically, had they come to the counselor of record, a far better solution would have been worked out. The grade for the first Environmental Studies course was in the seventies. The second Environmental Studies' average was in the mid-nineties. In light of the fact that the student would be applying for college the next year, it would have been far better for the student's GPA had the first course been dropped and the second kept for its high average. Instead, the transcript reflected a poor performance in the first course and lowered the GPA. Credits were not a consideration for this student; grades were.

Whom to Call List

All too often, the guidance counselor is called upon to supply information that really is not applicable to guidance and does not fall into the counselor's jurisdiction. This distracts counselors from their main tasks. A handy "**Whom to Call List**," which specifies whom to call and for what, should be drawn up. This list is different from the usual listing of personnel and departments. For example, calls for cap and gown information, senior trips, senior rings, etc., should not pass through the guidance office. The "**Whom to Call List**" should be published and circulated in various school documents. This will also save secretarial time. The most important step that should be taken before publishing the list is that each person responsible for a particular service (which is rightfully his or hers to begin with) accepts the assignment so designated. (See Addendum 3)

"Where's Charlie?"

Every school has custodians who perform valuable services for the guidance department. The same applies to hall monitors or teacher aids. Counselors should have a good working relationship with them. They are a main source of services and information. They, in many instances, have access to information that the counselor is unaware and if they are encouraged to share this information, the counselor is better informed. In addition, when the counselor is running a program, custodial staff usually performs the set up. A good working relation with them makes their willingness to assist so much easier.

It Takes Time

In this handbook, frequent mention is made to building relationships. This goal is something that only can be achieved over a period of time.

Principally, it is achieved in the counselor's daily contact with staff. If the counselor makes a conscious effort to relate meaningfully with staff, then in time, the results will build teamwork, yielding far better results for students.

Teachers Requesting
To Have Students Dropped from Their Class

If a teacher requests a student to be taken out of his/her class, be sure to process it properly with the teacher and department head. If it is for discipline or attendance, the assistant principal should be notified. Legitimate reasons are not limited to, but include: behavioral problems, the student has been misplaced academically, bullying, the student represents a major obstacle to other students' learning, etc. A teacher's preference does not constitute a valid reason. Class size is always a factor. In general, if a teacher sends a student to be dropped from his/her class, a drop form should be submitted with the rationale for the change and processed through the department head.

Parents Requesting to Switch a Counselor

No matter how kind, proficient, and well-intentioned counselors are, there will be occasions when students or parents will request a change of counselor. If it is an infrequent occurrence, then there is nothing to worry about. It maybe the chemistry between the counselor and the student or parent does not match, or a misrepresentation of the words that the counselor may have used. It happens to the best of counselors and should not be taken as a personal blow. However, if there are frequent requests to have students changed out of your caseload, then a real examination of the causes should be undertaken. Frequent switching is an indication of general dissatisfaction and administrators will not look very kindly on the causes. It could easily be one of the reasons for not granting tenure.

Verifying a Course Placement

There are times when the counselor is so busy he/she may fail to verify that a student is in the right course. A student's assessment and request for changing a course is not enough. It is imperative that the counselor checks the student's records before placing a student.

Keep in Touch

There are two key personnel in the building, who have a great deal of information relating to students. They are the school nurse and the attendance clerk. Both are privy to first hand information that is of real assistance to the counselor. There should be a mutual understanding that the counselor should be informed of any problems that might concern his/her students. To assume you will be informed is a mistake. Once again, a good relationship with these staff members facilitates communication. It is important that the counselor have immediate information on students who are seriously sick, injured, truant or constantly absent.

Befriend the Assistant Principals

A cordial relationship with assistant principals based on common interests is a valuable asset. So much information, disciplinary actions and parental contacts take place in the assistant principals' offices that they are a unique source of information for the counselor. They do not always have the time to communicate happenings or special circumstances to the counselor. Frequent contact with them serves as a means of increased communication. These contacts need not be formal. As assistant principals pass by in the hallway, are encountered in the cafeteria, or come to the guidance office on other matters, make it a point to recognize them. If they know you are interested in students and someone in particular, they will begin to share information.

Never Let Them Go

Whenever the counselor is on the phone with parents and they are dealing with a topic such as schedule changes, requests for information, college advice, etc., never terminate the conversation until you have covered the topic fully, thus eliminating the need for a follow up call. This will save the counselor time down the road and the counselor will know the parent is satisfied. Completing the topic saves the counselor a second phone call and avoids the possibility of forgetting to make the call. If the counselor has to get back to the parent and cannot supply the information immediately, the counselor should place a reminder in a follow up file.

Duplicating Materials

One of the busiest places in the building is the duplicating room (if there is one). Teachers and counselors may be lined up early in the morning to do their work. If the counselor has time later in the day to do the work and graciously allows other staff members ahead of him/her to do so, it is a sign to them that the counselor understands the tight schedules they have. This act of consideration will be returned in the future.

If your school has a person in charge of the duplicating room and the counselor has a good relationship with that person, it is amazing how quickly items will be returned to the counselor.

Counselors Are Subject to Criticism

Of all departments, the guidance department seems to be the one that is subject to the most criticism. The counselor's work is open to the greatest scrutiny and when a counselor makes a mistake, it usually is more costly than those of other staff members. Additionally, a counselor's work is less understood and often the only thing other staff members see are the perks: an office, an open schedule, and a telephone. Each time counselors speak with teachers, parents, administrators, and students they should let them in on the steps required to solve a particular problem. In this way a deeper appreciation and understanding of the counselor's work is established. A useful tool is occasionally to keep a log of your day's work. If the opportunity arises, it should be shared with administrators, teachers, and parents. (**Addendum 1.**)

Requirements for Out of District Placement

Before recommending students in the counselor's home building for an out of district placement, be sure they qualify. Each receiving school has its own qualifications for acceptance. It is unfair to recommend a placement for a student and later find out that the student does not meet the entrance requirements. Some schools require the student to be classified, while others do not. Some require a certain number of credits; others do not want disciplinary problems, etc. In addition, some school districts have a policy that requires all school personnel to get clearance from an administrator for an out of district recommendation, **before** making it. This is usually based on financial reasons.

Visit the Sites

Each school district has a number of placement sites wherein students whose needs are not being met in the home school are placed. Beginning counselors should visit these sites to learn their entrance requirements and the particular services they render. In this way, the counselor will have some knowledge of the new school he/she may be recommending. (As mentioned previously to administrators, a detailed orientation of new counselors should include such items as above.)

Tapping into Valuable Resources

Many times parents or students may ask the counselor to provide a tutor. This is not an easy task unless the counselor has resources available. If the school does not have a tutoring service, then the counselor may go to the National Honor Society and ask for a list of academically gifted students who might be willing to tutor a student in need. Another source is the counselor's own students, especially good students who need extra school activities for their resume. This list can be developed over a period of time as students come to see the counselor and the counselor inquires if they are willing to serve in the capacity of a tutor. Should the counselor moderate a club or team, members of the club are another good source.

Practical Implementation of a Tutoring Program

Simply to tell a student willing to tutor to contact another student in need is not sufficient. Days can go by before a contact is made. A more formal arrangement is necessary. Both students should be called to the guidance office at the same time, introduced to each other, and guidelines established:

1. What days will they meet?
2. Where they will meet?
3. For how long?
4. How to contact each other if an appointment cannot be kept?
5. What is the content to be covered?
6. Who will give the follow up report to the counselor?
7. The tutor should report the hours spent tutoring so that service hours may be recorded.

This becomes an additional motivational factor for the tutor.

Be Aware of a Good Thing

There are times when students will give a gift to a teacher or counselor before the end of the school year. All districts have a policy on this, which should be followed. If counselors are allowed to accept the gift, it is better to advise the student that you are not at liberty to receive the gift. This is especially applicable to students who are in danger of failing or have disciplinary problems. In this way, the teacher and the counselor may avoid a conflict of interest.

Birthdays

A nice touch in counseling is to remember a student's birthday. This difficult task can be made easy. Ask your computer expert for a list of your students by their birthdays. If you have a student aid or volunteer who works with you, have them fill out a calendar with all the birthdays listed. Make one of his/her jobs to inform you each day whose birthday it is. The benefits of this method are that if you meet the student in the hallway or are dealing with the student that day, you can easily wish him/her happy birthday. Word gets home that you know the student and have an interest in him/her. Some counselors are so organized that they have birthday cards made up and sent to the student on their birthday. Once again, a volunteer student-worker can facilitate this whole project. The counselor just has **to be organized and want to do it**. The student volunteer can do the rest. This procedure can apply to so many other good things the counselor can do, as mentioned before: filing, inspirational sayings, helping secretaries, compiling surveys, etc.

Be Creative

Counselors can become so busy that they hardly have time for incoming freshman. At the same time, one of the worst criticisms for a counselor to hear is, "I don't know who my counselor is," or "I never see my counselor." Whenever the occasion arises at either at an orientation session or a classroom visit, concentrate on making a lasting impression. This can be done either through your humor, some special talent you might have or by a creative gimmick, that gets your students' attention and by which they will remember you. A boring description of the services the counselor provides is not what they are looking for. Students are looking for someone who understands, is human and open to their needs.

Anecdote

One year a particularly inventive counselor put his face on a ten-dollar bill and ran off copies. As part of his orientation presentation to freshman students, the counselor promised that he would redeem the counterfeit with a real one in June of their senior year. This was his way of getting students to remember their counselor. Four years later as June rolled around, five students came to him for payment. Many more had lost the original (as the counselor had hoped.) Of the five students, some actually kept the counterfeit in their wallet for four years. It was a costly way to have his students remember him. This is not a recommended practice....but it was creative and it worked.

Yet another counselor did magic tricks at the orientation session, inquiring how a counselor is like a magician. (Both make things disappear.) Another did a memory trick. It is these kinds of gimmicks that students remember early on and will recall when they see the counselor passing in the hallway and will say hello. When a counselor has hundreds of students to care for, it is very helpful when students are proactive with their greetings.

Whom to Ask

There are times when asking the right person will get the best results for students. Asking the wrong person may not generate a negative answer but will certainly delay the outcome. At no point can the counselor go beyond the chain of command, but there are choices. Given the choice of directing a student to the school psychologist or the school social worker, experience will indicate the more effective person. Given the choice of asking the dean of discipline or a department head how to handle a difficult classroom situation, always choose the one who will bring about change. This kind of knowledge can only come with experience, but until then, seek advice from your fellow counselors.

What to Wear

The importance of being culturally aware applies to how a counselor will dress to serve the community. There are many considerations:

1. How do I dress to relate to students?
2. How do I dress to gain the respect and confidence of parents?
3. How do I dress for professional meetings or parent-student conferences?

This is quite a challenge since on the one hand parents expect counselors to be mature, have the experience and knowledge of their profession and, at the same time, someone who can relate to their child. Ultimately, it is a decision that the counselor must make based on sound judgment and knowledge of the cultural values of the community.

The Bell System.

Something as simple as memorizing the bell schedule for classes can become quite a useful tool. Teachers have no problem with this practice since they have to be on time for the start of each class. Some counselors never take the time or effort do so. It is a great time saver when the counselor who is away from his/her desk knows how much time is left in a period. If a counselor is aware of the time when each period is about to begin and he/she has an appointment, there is less likelihood that the counselor will show up late for the appointment with a parent or student.

A REMINDER

There are so many suggestions in this handbook that the beginning counselor may seem overwhelmed, and feel it is impossible to do all that is recommended. As frequently indicated, time and experience will make their application more feasible. Hopefully, you will be in this profession for most of your career. Wisdom and implementation come in time. No need to rush.

"Dare to give true advice with all frankness." Cicero (As recommended by the eminent lecturer, Dr. John Hugo Maggio)

CHAPTER 16

Counselor Organizational Skills

Organizing a Group Counseling Program

Many group-counseling sessions are unsuccessful because they are poorly organized. If the counselor expects the group to remain productive, the group must have two major components:

1. Students must have a common interest.

2. They must have mutual free periods or study halls in which to meet.

Setting up a Group-Counseling Program

1. With the aid of fellow counselors, compile a list of possible candidates, who fit the criteria for a group counseling session: children of divorced parents, grieving students, failing students, etc.

2. Check the list of names against the schedules of each student and see what free periods or study halls they have in common.

3. Submit a new list of students who have the same free periods to the counselors to selected groups for counseling based on specific topics. Cross off any students who would not work well in that particular group setting.

4. Approach students individually requesting them to participate in a group-counseling program and indicate the topic. Give them assurances that the group will be helpful and confidential. Students should receive a "Group Counseling Consent" form so that their parents can be aware that they will be in a group and can sign it before their group counseling session begins.

5. Set a specific time and date for the first meeting, well in advance. Then send a reminder to the students the day before the session begins. On the day of the first session, send out a guidance pass. These frequent reminders may seem like over-kill, however, it is very important that the first session be well attended. Once the group is set in motion, there is less need for reminders. At the first meeting, have some snacks to eat and drink as an icebreaker.

6. Set a time and date for the next meeting. The time and day for each meeting should be the same every week so that students will remember more easily.

7. Appoint or vote on a group leader whose responsibility will be to remind other members of the group of their next meeting.

8. On the morning of the next meeting, send out a reminder to each group member of the time and place for the meeting.

This method, though initially time consuming, will assure a group that is compatible, interested in the topic, and free at the same time to continue future sessions.

Find a Way

An effective counselor is an organized counselor. Every member of the school community agrees that the primary duty of the counselor is service to his/her students. There are two aspects to this service; one is clerical and the other is personal counseling. Of the two, personal service is regarded as primary. However, with today's emphasis on clerical accuracy in maintaining school records and schedules, computer input, and a variety of state mandates for information, the clerical aspect is becoming increasingly time consuming, even taking over, to the detriment of personal counseling. Each counselor must find a way to spend more time with students.

The Use of Binders

Counselors are responsible for keeping large amounts of paper information. It is recommended that they keep them in readily available binders by topic, or some other equally efficient filing method that works for the counselor. The advantage of binders is that grade levels can be divided into sections, facilitating the access to report cards, progress reports, and transcripts. Reports that are issued on a quarterly basis should replace previously issued reports. However, save all old reports in a special storage area for referral. There are many occasions when a grade is called into question or a grade has not been updated and the counselor needs the former reports. Separate binders may include:

1. Report cards
2. Progress reports
3. The master schedule
4. SSD accommodation information for students
5. BOCES information (or similar occupational programs)
6. Unofficial transcripts
7. Summer school grades
8. The "Follow Up" binder
9. College profiles binder
10. SAT, ACT score reports
11. International Baccalaureate binder
12. Telephone messages binder

13. Special student information binder.
14. Scholarship binder
15. Etc.

Much of this information is bulky and may have to be stored in a library unit or across the back of the counselor's desk, hence the utility of binders, which will put the information at the counselor's fingertips. Binders also help the counselor quickly organize incoming information. When counselors are unavailable, secretaries find it useful to know where the binders are kept to retrieve information as needed. (Another use of student volunteers is keeping those binders, which are not confidential, up to date.)

> *"Consistency, thou art a jewel." Proverb*
> (As quoted from the Memoirs of Marian Murphy)

Prioritizing

When the counselor is bombarded by multiple demands, the art of prioritizing becomes a necessity. A simple task such as checking and turning in grade changes that have occurred over the summer becomes a matter of prioritizing. To start at the ninth grade and work through to the twelfth seems logical. However, the counselor has to keep in mind that senior transcripts have to be finalized by the end of September. Parents and senior students must first have an opportunity to check their transcripts before they are sent to colleges. Handing in ninth grade changes first before handing in those for the twelfth grade is not to deal with the immediate needs of seniors.

Clerical Assistance

It is essential that the counselor obtain help filling, collating, etc. in order to minimize the time spent on clerical chores and free up the counselor to concentrate on matters of substance. (See Chapters 7 and 15 for more suggestions)

Student Information

In the case where a new counselor has assumed a former counselor's caseload, there are a number of sources/resources for obtaining information, including:

1. The anecdotal folders of the former counselor if left to the new counselor
2. The school psychologist
3. The school social worker
4. The cumulative folders
5. School administrators
6. The dean of discipline
7. The attendance officer
8. The school nurse

Each of the above personnel has knowledge about specific students. They will be happy to bring the counselor up to speed on students' school performance of a non-confidential nature. Present these personnel with a list of your counselees for their review. With the list, supply a code to simplify transferring information:

1. Fails to do home work.….. F
2. Disruptive in class.………..D
3. Personal family problems..P
4. Chronic absences.……….. A
5. Etc.,

When there is no problem, a blank entry is sufficient. Be proactive and initiate these contacts before students get in trouble, begin to fail, act out, etc.

Develop Quick Note Taking Skills

Counselors should be able to take notes quickly. Each student should have a folder in which an entry is easily made. Lengthy notations, though valuable, are time consuming and eventually lead to overload. In addition, the counselor should set up a file for lists that single out students for various reasons which emanate out of various offices: assistant principal, attendance, teachers, department heads, etc. These communications, which single out students, will prove invaluable in backing up any case or comment the counselor may have to make to a student, parent, or administrator.

Analyze Requests

Many people will ask the counselor to do things that do not come under the guidance umbrella. Be able to clarify your role and redirect the request. For example, when parents phone the counselor to deliver a message or a book or lunch to a student, respectfully refer them to the main office or to "**The Whom to Call List**" where they have personnel designated for such a purpose. Once the counselor agrees to these requests, parents will expect him/her to do it all the time.

Shifting the Load

This topic has been addressed previously. It bears repeating especially to help new counselors in their enthusiasm and willingness to please, from taking on too much extra work. One of the skills the counselor must develop is the art of saying "no" diplomatically. It can be done easily if a reasonable explanation is given. A common occurrence among counselors is a request for services by teachers and department heads to do things that they themselves should do: making phone calls that pertain only to their areas or setting up meetings that they should set up. Counselors may be asked to attend the meeting requested by a teacher, not asked to organize it. For example, some teachers do not feel at ease initiating and being present at a conference without someone acting as a buffer. In this case, the counselor should attend but all the prep work in organizing it is still the obligation of the teacher. If the counselor initiates the meeting, then the counselor organizes it. (In all cases, whatever school policy dictates in the above matters, it must be followed.)

There are some cases where it is the obligation of the teacher to set up the meeting. However, if the counselor feels the teacher is overloaded and volunteers to do the task, it is good public relations. But, as always, it should be clearly understood that the counselor is taking on the teacher's responsibility.

Getting Support

It is to the counselor's advantage to take on interns. They are bright and willing. Interns learn quickly and can be taught to do scheduling, college searches, make phone calls, etc. This will free up the counselor for other chores while the interns are working under the counselor's directives

RESULTS
Is this not what everything is all about?
Is this not what your goals are for?
Is this not what your life is all about?
The result proves the right way to live.
The result is the positive proof of the
Right solution and method. Alfred A. Montapert
(As researched by Professor Betty Cardone)

CHAPTER 17

Follow up File

Calendars

Counselors should consider keeping a separate calendar for after school events and refer to it periodically so they do not miss special events. Marking the calendar supplied by the school or your computer calendar is a good resource for after school appointments. For daily appointments, the guidance secretary usually supplies the following information: student appointments, in-school meetings, parent conferences, etc. Two separate calendars help the counselor to divide the day in two. The after school calendar is for professional meetings, conferences, night meetings and personal appointments and can be checked out days ahead without any confusion.

Date Everything

Whenever the counselor sends a document to be completed by another staff member or department head, be sure to date when the material was sent and returned. This will cover the counselor if there are any unreasonable delays in the processing of the document. A request by a parent to have a student classified by the CSE, should take place in at least thirty school days. When the counselor dates his/her part of the document, there will be no culpability if the process extends beyond the time limit. The same applies when parents, the principal, the courts, etc. ask the counselor for special documents. A handy tool is a rubber stamp which indicates the date.

"At Risk Students"

Counselors cannot remember all their students who are "at risk." These students are in most need of the counselor's attention. However, "at risk students" can easily be lost in the shuffle of the counselor's demanding schedule. Keep a separate list of these "at risk students" so that you can check on them periodically. This list should be in your follow up folder, file, binder, etc.

"It's not enough to help the feeble up,
But to support him after." Shakespeare
(As exemplified by Viola Readon)

Follow Up Calls

When students have a need for special arrangements, a follow up call is necessary. Calls should be made if there is:

1. The need for a medical bus for an injured student
2. A problem at BOCES (occupational center)
3. A request by a student to advocate for him/her with a college
4. A request by a parent for teacher reports
5. Any follow up call to another professional
6. Calls that encourage students that are sick or have a family tragedy.
7 Etc.

Again, regarding any of the above, a reminder should be placed in the follow up file.

Requesting Transcripts

Concerning transcripts for any incoming students, the counselor should phone the prior school and request that transcripts be sent. Be sure to follow up. Mark your progress in you follow-up folder. Do not let time slip by so that the student ends up without any grades on the transcript. When the sending school indicates it will get the information to the counselor, never take it for granted. The sending school can easily overlook forwarding the transcript information.

Request Student Information

At the intake interview of transferring students, parents are not always open as to the true reason for the transfer. They hope, with a fresh start, everything will turn out fine. However, if the student has some family problem, a discipline problem, is a student at academic risk or classified, it is important for the counselor to know. It usually takes some probing on the part of the counselor before the parent will open up. If this does not occur, a follow up call to the sending school is necessary.

Case Study

A particular young woman, who happened to be six feet, two inches tall and had a very strong build, transferred into a new school. Everyone was excited about the prospect of her potential as a basketball player. As it turned out, she had a violent streak and within a few days, she was found fighting in the hallway, with extreme brutality, injuring several female students. The principal was quite upset that the young woman was allowed into the building. Fortunately, the counselor had followed up and called the student's previous school and had passed the information on to the assistant principal.

Classification Denied

There will be times when transferring students are classified as special education students and the parents do not wish to share this information with the counselor. Some parents feel it is not necessary or that they do not want the student to begin the new school with a "stigma." If the counselor picks this up, a discussion on the pros and cons of this approach should be held with the parent. Once again, the follow up with the student's former counselor is crucial to evaluating this kind of information.

Folders

It is recommended always to keep two divisions in the **follow-up** binder or folder:

1. Long term: courses or requests that the student needs for next year

2. Short term: for immediate follow up as required.

Lost Messages

In the course of a counselor's busy day, many messages of importance come cross his/her desk. If you are familiar with what a counselor's desk looks like, you know it is generally filled with all kinds of papers. It is imperative to develop the habit of filing these messages immediately. A major concern of counselors is the loss of important messages. Get into the habit of placing these items in specific area, file, folder, etc. This habit assures the counselor of not losing any important requests or messages. It is very embarrassing when the counselor is called to task for not getting back to an administrator or parent because of a lost message.

Counselor Reminders

When the counselor meets students in the hallway and they give him/her a request or a job to take care of, always tell the students to write the request down and give it to the guidance secretary. In this way, the counselor will not forget the request or lose the paper it was written on in the course of the day. Additionally, the counselor is placing the responsibility back on the student and the counselor cannot be held responsible if the student does not follow through.

Secretarial Reminders

A habit to instill in secretaries is to have them remind the counselor of important meetings, conferences, chores, etc. Once secretaries know the counselor's style, they will begin to remind the counselor automatically.

Get into the Habit

It is a great idea to have a follow up folder. But, unless the counselor makes it a habit to place follow up information in the folder, it is meaningless. This is especially so if the counselor is in the middle of another task and says to him/herself, "I'll be sure to do it later."

"Good order is the foundation of all good things."
Edmund Burke (As suggested by Genevieve Burbank)

CHAPTER 18

College Planning

"Climb the Highest Mountain"

For parents who are beginning the college process for the first time, the task may seem "in sur **mount** able." (Pardon the pun but it is the only way to tie in the college planning process with the beautiful mountain picture captured by Paul Caravelli.) But like the mountain, the college process can be fun to climb. At first, there are feelings of being overwhelmed, confused, and frustrated. The job of the counselor is to allay these fears and map out a timely plan for completion of the application process. Not everything has to be done at once and the counselor's step-by-step instruction will make a seemingly daunting task more feasible.

RICHARD O'CONNELL, ED. D.

The Sum of All the Parts

The college planning process is a long and complicated one. It need not be an arduous process if the counselor, parent, and student address each issue in a timely fashion. College planning is an integral part and the summation of a twelfth grader's education. The counselor's job is to assist the parents and student in presenting the student's academic and personal achievements in the best possible light to each college admissions committee. This task covers a whole range of topics:

from writing essays
to planning the résumé,
from recommending colleges,
to advising different strategies on marketing the student,
from coaching for interviews and personal contacts,
to advising on what to expect in college, etc.

Since each student is different, each situation presents a unique and special challenge.

Begin Early

In dealing with high-powered students as well as average students, it is important in middle school and even in the earlier grades, to direct students to meaningful activities that can significantly influence their college acceptance in their senior year. Colleges do not necessarily look for a long list of school activities. Rather, they are more concerned with the student's staying power and achievements in a particular activity. It is extremely important to note that high achievement in one area is more important than multiple activities. In the matter of after school activities, the student should specialize. The more unique the achievement is, the better. Colleges are looking to fill special niches in compiling a freshman class that is both gifted and diversified. (See Addendum 12)

Unrealistic Aspirations

When parents and their student come for a college conference and have high expectations that are unrealistic, never initially dampen these aspirations. The counselor need not be the bearer of bad news but should begin the self-education process of the student and parent. Refer the parents and student to the profiles of the colleges that they have expressed an interest. Let them read the profiles and see what academic parameters the colleges are requesting. Profiles may be obtained through the college's web site, publications, admissions office, etc. Profiles provide a realistic assessment, eliminating the need for the counselor's direct response. Gradually, parents will come to a true assessment of the student's college potential and the counselor will be able to serve as helper and not as a doom's day counselor. The counselor also avoids the infamous complaint, "My counselor put me down and said I could never get into..." **(See sample profiles in Addendum 4.)**

During the course of time, counselors can build up a binder wherein are placed multiple profiles. It is a handy binder to share with parents if they are interested in obtaining an overview of various college acceptance requirements.

Other Factors

If a counselor is dealing with students who fall below the academic parameters of a specific college, there are other mitigating factors, which may support the student's candidacy. Outstanding qualities, skills, or achievements that are of significant merit will enter into the equation. Stressing these strengths and talents may provide **hope** for entering a specific college. These achievements must, however, be clearly defined in the student's recommendation and validated with some form of proof: articles, awards, videos, CD's, DVD's, test scores, etc.

Senior Questionnaire

Early in the senior year, a helpful tool for the counselor is a questionnaire for seniors. In it, they are asked to supply a list of colleges where they intend to apply, their intended major, their extracurricular activities and community volunteer efforts. They may also indicate if they are entering the military or the work force. Once all the seniors have filled out the questionnaire, the information from the questionnaire should be collated and placed in a binder.

Colleges indicated by students will be placed alphabetically in the binder and under each college will be listed all the names of students who have chosen that particular college. The counselor will then have a list of all the students who are applying to specific colleges. Keeping such a list of all students applying to a specific college will make it easier for the counselor to gather these students when college representatives come to the school.

The same method applies for college majors, and volunteer activities. The name of each senior is listed under a specific college major as well as each volunteer activity. This will assure that the counselor will have the information readily available when the need arises. For example, when a scholarship comes in for someone majoring in engineering or architecture, the information is right there. If a scholarship comes in for someone who has volunteered in a hospital, the same applies. This information is also valuable at the end of the year when the counselor is asked to recommend or nominate students for special school scholarships. Once the counselor has collated such information, a practical procedure is to give the guidance secretary the binder of information. When a visiting college is expected, the secretary simply checks the book and sends for students to meet with the representative.

The counselor may ask, "When will I have time for all this collating?" The answer once again is the use of students to collate this information. It is another good example of how to use student volunteers and save the counselor time. The counselor just has to be organized to set the plan in motion. Again, sharing this technique with other counselors is another good example of teamwork. A sample questionnaire is in **Addendum 6.** A generous act upon the part of the counselor, which is appreciated by fellow counselors, is to organize the distribution and collection of these questionnaires for all seniors. A student volunteer, once again, can handle the collating of the questionnaires for each counselor. Secretaries are appreciative as well.

Visiting Colleges

There are certain guidelines the counselor should recommend to students for making a good college visit:

1. Call ahead and get an appointment. Plan to spend half a day at each college.
2. Cluster the colleges so that you do not spend an inordinate amount of time traveling.
3. Visit the dorms; see their condition and the male/female arrangements.
4. Stay over night, if possible, with an alumnus of your high school.
5. Talk to students on campus.
6. Make specific appointments with athletic or department personnel.

Remember that even a bad visit can be worthwhile by providing a basis for comparison. Now the student's mind will be more focused as to what she/he may actually want in a college. Also, remember that no college is perfect. Colleges are like human beings. They have a personality and an orientation uniquely their own. Like human beings, they have their faults and strong points. Most decisions to attend a particular college are based on compromise. Seldom is there a perfect match.

Anecdote

The benefit of visiting college campuses is that parents and students get to see things that they could never have anticipated. On one occasion, a young female tour guide was taking a parent and her daughter through her dorm area when an Adonis walked out of the shower room half clad, wrapped with only a towel around his waist. He went into the room opposite the tour guide's room. Depending on the orientation of the family, this could be a major concern, which should be addressed immediately. Does the college have separate dorm buildings for men or woman, or alternating floors for men and women? Likewise, in the matter of academics, does the college provide dorms that are more academically oriented as opposed to an open dorm with no restrictions or curfew hours.

Alternate Visits

There are circumstances in families, either financial or personal, where they cannot take long trips to visit colleges. It is good advice to instruct students to visit local colleges that may be similar in type to the schools they have targeted. At least these students and parents will have the experience of being on a similar campus.

Other types of visits can be made:

1. By obtaining a video DVD or CD from the college or school library

2. By contacting students at the interested college

3. By phoning the college directly and speaking to an admissions counselor

4. By contacting alumni

5. By obtaining specific written and printed information from the college

6. By consulting various college guides

7. By speaking to the home school counselor about colleges

8. By searching the internet

After the College Visit

When making a college visit, the counselor should be sure to advise the student to write down the name of the person who interviewed him/her, or if an interview cannot be had, get the name of the director of admissions. Upon returning home, the student should write a "thank you" note to whoever took the time to meet with him/her and indicate that he/she will be applying. This will help the student from becoming a face with no identity on the college application. After the application has been sent and a period of time has elapsed, the student should make a direct call asking pertinent questions. Student phone contacts are placed in the student's folder. E-mails expressing continued interest as well as clippings, videos, CD's, etc. of the student's latest accomplishments are important. It is well to realize that some colleges want students to express a real interest. Above all, the student must do all the work. College admission personnel are astute at recognizing when an application packet is prepared by the parent or a professional and not the student. (On all materials sent to colleges, be sure to place your Social Security number. This is usually the method used by colleges to organize their files.)

Anecdote

Recently, two students, who fell slightly below the academic requirements of an Ivy League and a "Little Ivy" college, were both accepted. The principal reason for their acceptance was their personal, constant contact with a specific admissions person who had interviewed him/her either on campus or on a school visit. The students were able to impress the admission officers with their personal qualities, extra curricular achievements, academic performance, etc. Once the contact was made, it was sustained.

Who Makes the Call?

In all matters that pertain to the student, the student must be the one to contact college personnel.

Anecdote

One very industrious mother took the counselor's advice to contact colleges, but ignored the advice that the student makes the contact calls. Over a period of time, she called one of the military academies seven times for information and to show genuine interest. She found it very strange that her son, who seemed to have all the qualifications for acceptance, was denied. Parents have to realize that each time they call, it is recorded in the student's application folder. Apparently, the academy considered the young man to be "a mama's boy" with no personal initiative. He was denied accordingly.

Counselors Visiting Colleges

As is important as it is for students to visit colleges, it is more important that counselors make college visits. There are many students who do not have the finances to do so. If counselors make annual outings to different colleges, they build a vast reservoir of first hand information and can share their findings with parents and students. The information gained through college visits is vital, as are the college contacts. If the counselor knows the admission officer personally, it is a real asset for future students. No matter how limited the guidance budget, it is a great disservice to students having counselors on staff with limited first hand knowledge of the colleges to which most of their students usually applies.

The Ivies

If a counselor has a high-powered student applying to an Ivy League university or another high-powered college and the district allows counselors to make college visits, it is well to plan a visit to that university. Significant goals can be achieved. It establishes a personal contact with the Ivy League admissions officer, allowing the counselor to share the merits of a superior student. Nothing impresses an admissions officer more than a personal, on campus visit of a counselor advocating for a student. This procedure cannot be done in every case. However, once the contact is made, it will help other students as well.

Campus Security

If parents have concerns about college campus security, they should go on the internet and check out the college's police report. Parents should reserve judgment until they check out other colleges. Colleges are like small cities, and as such, they will have instances of crime, that must be reported. Hence, a comparative study is required before making a final judgment.

The College Interview

If a student has an interview, the counselor should provide the following advice: the student should tour the campus first; read the school newspaper, eat in the cafeteria, visit the dorms, etc. Bring as much knowledge of the college to the interview as possible. Admissions officers can detect and appreciate the preparedness and genuine desire of a student to attend their college. Likewise, the counselor should coach the student that during the course of the interview:

1. Be relaxed; remember that the admissions officer you are speaking to is as anxious to make a good impression. His/her job at this point is to market the college. Later, they will begin to discriminate in the acceptance process.

2. College admissions personnel do not expect students to wear a Brooks Brothers suit. They also do not appreciate a student who arrives disheveled and half-asleep.

3. Even if the student has not made up his/her mind about the college, it is wise to show as much enthusiasm as possible to the admissions officer.

4. The student should have specific questions to ask and try to anticipate some of the interviewer's questions.

5. If the student cannot have a personal interview, he/she should obtain the name of the college admissions officer responsible for his/her region and make contact.

6. The student should have specific questions about the **college major** he/she is interested in and the reasons why he/she may want to attend that college. The more specific and informed the student is about the college's offerings, the more admissions personnel will be impressed.

Case Studies

A young lady had applied to a prestigious college and within that college to a very specialized program. After the interview, she was informed that she was rejected. The cause for this denial was not that she did not have good grades, but that she did not demonstrate a real knowledge of what the specialized college had to offer. She had not done her homework and had not investigated the courses that were offered and how they would fit into her career goal. The college wanted her to ask questions beyond general inquiries and show a real insight into the curriculum and courses offered in their specialized college program.

Another young man was surprised by the following question from an admissions counselor, "Tell me about your special failings as an individual?" The student had enough presence of mind to turn this question to his advantage by saying that he is very meticulous about his work which causes him, at times, to be rushed at the final deadline. He followed up by indicating that his work was always thorough and well researched and generally of a higher quality than other students' work.

Special Education Students and College

All the information supplied in this chapter applies to special education students. For more information on special education students applying to college, see "Guidance and the Special Education Student," **Chapter 6.**

College Reps

Whenever college admissions personnel visit the high school, the counselor has the opportunity to make meaningful contacts. Some schools position the admissions personnel out in the hallway and barely pay any attention to them. Every effort should be made to make them welcome. Obtain their business card; learn the college's principal majors and the attributes of the college. (Develop an alphabetical file of business cards for easy referral.) Whenever the counselor can, he/she should maintain contact with these reps and build a college file of admission counselors for quick reference. Building personal relationships with college admission personnel is a gradual process that will prove extremely useful when the counselor has to advocate for a student. Admissions officers welcome the personal touch and the warm reception they receive at your school. Some schools have specific days when several colleges are invited. A real effort to extend a welcome to them with coffee and cookies, etc. is long remembered. The interest and welcome they experience at your school will pay off.

College File

Visiting admission personnel will usually visit the guidance office with a bundle of material for the counselor. Should counselors attempt to keep a file of this material in their office, it will quickly become overwhelming. Most guidance offices have a central filing area. Do not become a collector unless you have a great deal of space to store files and someone to do your filing.

Notify the Counselor

If a student e-mails the college application over the internet and fails to notify his/her guidance counselor, the student may receive an incomplete application notice. This is due to a failure on the part of the student to request the forwarding of his/her official transcript, letters of recommendation, resume and other pertinent information from the guidance office. At times, the student may notify the counselor and still get a notice of incompletion. The transcript and the notice may have crossed in the mail. A simple call to the college admissions office can clarify this difficulty.

Marketing

In the business world, the concept of marketing is crucial. Once again, if a student is interested in a specific college, every effort to express interest in that college and to add any additional information to his/her application should be made.

1. The counselor should encourage students to e-mail college reps, or for additional emphasis, to phone is better. Some colleges have well over 20,000 applicants, making it all the more essential for a student to personalize him/herself.

2. Students should request additional information; it is a sign of genuine interest.

3. If a teacher who has written a recommendation for a student receives an award, send the information on the teacher to the student's colleges.

4. Students should send newspaper clippings, special awards, or achievements as they occur to be added to the application packet.

5. If the student has not made a personal campus visit, do so and make it a point to see the contact person.

Anecdote

Two students applied to the same prestigious college. One had a 96 average and the other had a 94. They were similar in all aspects, except the student with the 94 average made a special trip to visit the campus and speak with an admissions officer. The same student continued to demonstrate interest by sending additional material. Of the two, the one who made the visit and had the lower average was accepted.

Decline Other Acceptances

When students are accepted into a college and are certain of their college choice, it is a courtesy to notify the other colleges of their decision. This helps these colleges open spaces for other students.

Web Sites

Each guidance department should develop an effective web site that lists: graduation requirements, SAT, ACT test dates, check lists and links to course offerings, scholarships, financial aid, career information, college searches, etc. It is a great referral source for parents and admissions counselors to learn general information about the school through the school profile.

Anecdote

School Profiles

Every high school should have its own profile that is enclosed in the college application packet. Upon making a college visit, a counselor was surprised when the admissions counselor pulled out a binder and made specific reference to the information supplied by his school. Admissions committees do categorize high schools and their academic performance as they accept various students from a particular high school. Their decision is largely based on the information found in the school profile.

Enthusiasm in the College Planning Session

In the student-parent-college planning meeting, the counselor should show real enthusiasm. If the student is prepared, focused, and involved, all the better. This demonstrates satisfaction on the counselor's part and is complimentary to the student, which in turn further encourages the student in a difficult process. For those less involved, a more step-by-step approach is necessary, with even more enthusiasm. A counselor's positive attitude goes a long way towards encouraging students to overcome the difficulties standing in the way of going to college.

Teach Compromise

During the college planning conference, counselors may run into a situation where the parent wants one type of college and the student wants another. In such cases, it is well to indicate that this is the wrong time for an argument. (Arguments are to be saved for when the student is accepted into a college.) Each should agree to send applications to a range of colleges that satisfy both. The outcomes at this point are all speculative and will really depend on whether the student is accepted. It is too early for this type of unnecessary argument. It is analogous to a fisherman going out to sea and casting out his net. You can only eat the fish you catch and it makes no sense to be concerned with those that get away.

Master College Chart

It is a worthwhile practice, after the counselor has given students their first list of possible colleges, for students to make a master chart. On this chart, colleges are listed in the vertical column and topics of concern are listed horizontally. For example, across the top could read: tuition, location, dorms, food, college major, safety, SATs, etc. Each college can then be rated. There is no perfect choice or perfect college. The Master Chart can assist the student in weighing the strong and weak points of various colleges by rating the college according to how it meets the student's needs. It is well to mention that the final decision can come only after students have been accepted into several colleges. Revisit these colleges (if possible), and discuss the pros and cons with parents and then come to an agreement.

The College Essay

What parents and some paid college advisors sometimes forget is that the people who review the college applications are professionals. They are highly trained in what to expect. They can spot an essay that is not genuinely the result of the student's effort. They have plenty of material before them in the application that indicates the student's capabilities and can see if the student's academic performance matches the skills exhibited in the essay.

Some Suggestions on the College Essay

A thought to keep in mind is that the readers who review the essay have literally hundreds to do in a day. If they allot 10-15 minutes per application, let alone an essay, it is generous. Consequently, the primary thought the student should have in mind is to be original, catch the reader's attention and make a lasting impression. Banal topics or the same old approach should be avoided. Some colleges will give a choice of topics. This makes it all the more difficult since the student's essay must stand out. A catchy beginning and a well thought out and constructed essay to supplement an interesting topic should be the student's objective.

Timing of the College Essay and Resume

The student should work on the college essay and resume over the summer. When the student returns in September, he/she should seek assistance from the English teacher and tap into a program the high school has set up for this very purpose. If there is no set procedure for assistance, the counselor and PTA should advocate for one. In some high schools, the college essay and resume are the first part of the senior year English course.

The Common Application

A great tool in the application process is the Common Application. It saves an enormous amount of time and if done on the internet, much replication of paper work is avoided. It lists over two hundred colleges, including those colleges that require a supplement, which may be another essay. Students should not forget to forward a check if they have not supplied a credit card number. As noted, transcripts, recommendations, resumes, and special materials should be requested to be sent from the high school guidance office.

Deadlines for College Admissions

A good source for finding out college application due dates is to look on the Common Application. Students may also go online to www. Collegeboard.com to obtain this kind of information or go to the actual college web site. College web sites usually follow a similar pattern, www. (the name of the college) followed by .edu

Application Cover Page

Students submitting college applications to the guidance counselor for forwarding should be required to include **A College Application Check List**, prepared by the guidance department and filled in by the student. This will obviate several possible problems, affording the student one final opportunity to carefully check to make sure the application is properly filled out and complete. **(Addendum 5.)**

It should contain:

1. Name of college
2. Date application was handed in
3. How the student is applying (online/hardcopy)
4. How the student is paying the application fee (check or credit card)
5. Deadline date for filing
6. SAT or ACT scores, if the school includes them in the application

Many colleges require the SAT or ACT scores be sent directly from the testing center.

7. Parental signature

8. Student's signature waiving the right to read letters of recommendation

9. Counselor's signature

10. Date sent from the guidance department

Tracking College Applications

Another useful tool for the counselor is to make the student include stamped two post cards in the application packet; one mailed back to the guidance office and the other addressed back to the student. The college will use them to indicate if anything is missing. The importance of this tracking procedure is evident when students come to the counselor's office and claim the college never received all the required information in the application from the guidance office. The first post card assures that the student has covered all the bases. The second post card mailed back to the school, assures the counselor that he/she has also forwarded all required information. (**Addendum 5.**) In this way, both the student and the counselor will have a quick indicator from the college as to what is required to complete the application. Some colleges take a very long time to notify students that something is missing; others may not get around to it due to the large number of applicants. Some schools may have these post cards printed up for convenience of the students.

Anecdote

A parent notified the counselor that five applications were sent to colleges by overnight mail to meet the deadlines. A request was then made of the counselor to send five transcripts and supporting materials the very next day. (No consideration was given as to the imposition this might pose on the counselor and his/her appointment schedule.) Even though the counselor sent the transcripts, essay, resume, and recommendations out in time to meet the deadline, the process of matching up the sent application with the high school records could take weeks on the college level. When colleges have thousands of applications, matching takes a while. In this case, since the two components each arrived separately the application was not considered completed. The student as such missed the deadline. The time delay in matching the application and the supporting material prevented the application from being read at the beginning of the process. The parent inquired of the counselor why the deadlines were not met. The counselor went to great lengths to explain the bureaucratic steps involved in the college system for matching up and completing the filing of an application.

Documents and Applications

When students attempt to give the counselor documents or college applications that are incomplete, do not accept them until they are complete and ready to go. The guidance secretary should never allow seniors to drop off college applications in the counselor's mailbox. If the counselor accepts applications in the hallway and later places them on a file cabinet, the counselor will probably forget them and miss the deadline. Always place the responsibility on the student to complete his/her work before handing it directly to the counselor in his/her office. Students are notorious for forgetting to complete applications. Let it be their responsibility to complete everything. The counselor should never accept anything in the hallway or allow students to drop the application on his/her desk before the counselor can review and access the application. In the first case, it can be lost and in the second, it may be incomplete.

Have a Place for the Application

There are special instances when a counselor may accept an incomplete application from a student. The application may be complete but the student may be waiting for a teacher recommendation and the counselor will store the application somewhere.

The secret for the counselor is
       to store it in a safe place,
          the same place
,   all the time.

While it may be more convenient to store it in the outer office senior college file, the difficulty with this is that it is easy to forget it is there and miss a deadline. If the counselor stores it consistently in his/her special draw, it will be more visible and easier to keep track of deadlines. Likewise, tell the secretary where you store incomplete college applications. If the counselor is sick or the secretary wants to add something to it such as a recommendation, she knows where to look.

The Secret to Success

In the college application process, it is highly recommended that students be trained
　　to submit
　　　　on the same day
　　　　　　in the same package
　　　　　　　all materials
　　　　　　　　　　necessary to complete the application.

NCAA Guidelines for Athletes

Counselors should be sure to have their student athletes, who are considering playing for Division I-II sports, register with the NCAA. The form can be found on-line www.ncaa.org Most importantly, counselors should check that all the NCAA academic requirements are in place. If a student becomes ineligible due to a failure to take required academic courses, real problems will arise.

Athletic Information

The packaging of all pertinent information for a college coach's review should be done well in advance. The high school coach working with the student usually helps in the preparation of the athletic material. At times, the college coach will request a transcript and say he/she will send the applicant's information to the admissions office. The counselor and the student should not regard this as sufficient. A formal application with all supporting material should also be sent from the guidance office directly to the admissions office.

Admissions Fee Waivers

One advantage of having a college coach involved in sending a transcript to the admissions department is that the coach can ask for a fee waiver. If the coach does not mention it, there is no harm in suggesting the possibility. This also applies to any student who cannot afford the application fee.

Marketing the Athlete

Marketing the student athlete follows many of the patterns for marketing Ivy League students. However, in regards to the timing, the process should begin much earlier to give college coaches sufficient time to review tapes, CDs, newspaper articles, and even attend games to see the athlete perform.

Some suggestions:

1. The student should prepare a sports resume following the guidelines suggested above.

2. The student should prepare a cover letter expressing why he/she, the athlete, is interested in the college's sports program and listing most recent achievements. Additionally, if the student has an academic reason for attending the college, mention it.

3. Include tapes, CDs and newspaper articles, and upcoming game schedules

4. If possible, a personal contact from the student's high school coach is helpful.

5. The address and contact information of college athletic personnel can be found in the **National Directory of College Athletes,** (women's and men's edition) usually kept in the guidance office.

6. Be sure to file the NCAA form.

7. Be sure to do follow up with thank you letters

8. Send recent achievements and awards not in the original application as they occur.

9. Make an approved college visit.

Student Involvement

When reviewing college applications or SAT registration forms, have students actively check that all information is correct, and complete. Students have to assume responsibility for their documents and it is good training for the future. The counselor should then make a final comprehensive check.

Early Decision

All problems associated with choosing from several colleges are obviated by the choice of Early Decision. But, even this choice must be made maturely and after carefully weighing all options. It is a definite commitment that is not easily broken. There must be a justifiable reason to break the agreement. Additionally, although there is no need to send out other applications, a backup plan should exist if the early decision is negative. The advantage of the early decision process is that students are accepted months earlier (December vs. March) and this takes the pressure of waiting for a decision off the shoulders of the student. If Early Decision is the student's choice, she/he should be prepared to complete the application a month or so early. If this is the case, it is all the more important that teacher recommendations be requested well in advance of the Early Decision dead line date.

College Roommates

One of the reasons why students return home to continue their college education is the poor experience they have had with a college roommate. Most colleges have a computerized program that matches students by their interests, background, etc. Most colleges will give a questionnaire to entering freshman to determine an appropriate roommate. This is most helpful in matching compatible students. Usually the assigned roommate is identified well before the opening of school. It should be suggested to the student to get in touch with the new roommate(s) and begin a positive relationship. This also allows roommates to coordinate who brings what. This avoids duplication of such items as refrigerators, ironing boards, vacuum cleaners, TV's sets. If the match up does not work out and the chemistry is not right, the student should act as soon as possible to request a change from the resident director on campus.

Anecdotes

No matter how hard parents and students try to sort out the right roommate, unforeseen problems may arise:

1. There are cases where the roommate will invite his girl friend to stay over night to have sex on a continuous basis.

2. There are cases where the roommate turns out to be a drug addict.

3. Some roommates are dirty and sloppy, play loud music and stay up all night.

4. There are even cases where the roommate is emotionally unstable and will threaten their roommate.

BE INSISTENT WITH THE DIRECTOR OF RESIDENTIAL SERVICES AND HAVE A CHANGE MADE IMMEDIATELY.

Anticipate College Problems

Parents should be instructed to plan ahead and advise their son or daughter on what steps should be taken if she/he runs into the following situations:

1. An intolerable roommate
2. Campus meals that are horrendous
3. Harassment is a problem

4. Going off campus at night or walking alone on campus at night is dangerous

5. Handling money becomes a problem

6. Personal hygiene is a concern

7. Academic status is in jeopardy

8. Drugs and excessive alcohol becomes a problem

9. The dangers of date rape

10 Etc.

Anecdote

Going off to college and having all the bases covered is a great feeling. Parents, however, should be prepared for the unexpected. Something as unforeseen as mandated consumption of cafeteria food in the freshman year could pose a problem for someone who is used to healthy, wholesome, and flavorful home cooked meals. This is an important item in a student's life. **"An army travels on its stomach."** If the student is very studious or invests a great deal of time in athletics, one of the things he/she looks forward to is having something enjoyable to eat at the end of the day. Students should confer with their parents if this is not the case. If parents want their son or daughter to stay in college and not at their doorstep, they may have to invest in the Marshall Plan…SEND FOOD as the US did for Germany, etc. in the late forties. (Is the author dating himself here?) If this is not possible, come up with a plan for alternate sources of pleasurable eating.

Procrastination

In the whole college application process, from beginning to end, a personal habit of procrastination is self-defeating. At the beginning, late applications decrease changes of acceptance because of the large number of students who have applied earlier. After being accepted, failure to send in the acceptance fee may cause a cancellation of the acceptance.

Testing and Financial Aid

SAT's and ACT testing information as it relates to college applications can be found in **Chapter 23** on Testing. Additional information on Financial Aid is found in **Chapter 20.**

Preventing College Drop Outs

Every high school system, as well as colleges, has a major concern for its students' college retention rate. High schools are vitally interested in providing pro-active services, which will enable students to graduate from college. The following program is offered as a partial solution for small high school graduating classes or for specific "at risk students" in a large graduating class.

Steps in a College Preventative Drop Out Program

1. The counselor should explain and obtain permission from school authorities to have a preventative college drop out program.

2. Then, the counselor should canvas the local community for college graduates who would be willing to mentor, advise and encourage beginning college freshman. The volunteer mentors should submit to the counselor a resume, work and personal experiences, college they graduated from, background and phone information. It is a good practice to link, with mutual agreement, students planning to attend a mentor's former college.

3. The choice of a volunteer mentor is totally up to the graduating senior and his/her parents. Seniors will choose from the resumes; they may even know the volunteer mentor.

4. An interview session can then be set up to see if the senior and the volunteer mentor are compatible.

5. The advantages of having volunteer mentors with college experience as opposed to family members is that they are not authority figures, nor emotionally involved with the students. They can be more objective than parents and may be more open to topics that the student would not discuss with his/ her parents.

6. The parents should also be at the interview session. They too would have to approve the mentor. In the end, the decision to drop out of college would need parental input and approval.

7. There should be frequent contacts with the student and at least an annual personal meeting with the volunteer mentor to get an update on the student's progress. Volunteers would be encouraged to make a trip to the college as a demonstration of interest and concern. It would also provide a realistic assessment of whatever problem might be affecting the student.

8. This program is time consuming to set up and the counselor could enlist the help of a parent or a former student to volunteer to coordinate the program under the counselor's direction.

9. Annually, the counselor will review the records kept on each student's progress for statistical purposes.

10. A personal phone call by the counselor to each volunteer should be made periodically to encourage him/her in his / her four-year commitment.

This program is intended for counselors to implement. But for schools that do not have such a program, parents may improvise one of their own for their son or daughter. Likewise, if there is any other idea in the book that strikes the reader and would like to see it implemented, talk it over with the principal and the director of guidance at the same meeting to get proper feed back.

Be Prepared to Weep

Few parents can anticipate the sadness they will experience when their son or daughter leaves for college. These same emotions arise in the student as well. It is a first real parting and genuine emotions will rise to the surface. At rare times, this same strong feeling of being homesick will deeply affect their son or daughter, resulting in a request to return home. In this case, a compromise must be worked out. Staying for at least a full semester will generally solve the problem. However, if homesickness persists after the first semester, some action should be taken.

It is amazing, however, that after all the hassle about what college to choose and then coming to a final decision, the student will say after a few months at the college, "How could I have ever chosen another college? I'm so happy here." Have confidence that the final choice will work out fine.

Staying Home While Away

Students who board at colleges that are not far from their home will be tempted to return home for the weekend, especially if they have a boy/girl friend. This could be a bad habit to get into since it defeats the purpose of being away at college. The lessons of being independent, bonding with fellow college students, enjoying the activities of weekend college life, etc. are wasted. Such students miss the rhythm of college life and can begin to feel as if they are not part of the college.

Immunization Records

Be alerted that college bound students will have to supply a complete immunization record before they are admitted to the college

"The dearest hope of the parent for his child is that he/she becomes all that he/she is capable of being. This is precisely the goal of school and college and exactly what city, state, and nation strive for." Dr. Morris Meist (As suggested by Patty Ann Anderson)

CHAPTER 19

College Recommendations

Objectivity

O ne of the most difficult tasks for the counselor is writing the college recommendation, especially when 60 to 100 have to be produced. The counselor must be well organized and informed to do justice to this task. Of paramount consideration is that each student is showcased to the maximum. This is difficult at times since some students do not always put their best foot forward during high school, resulting in academic or disciplinary problems. Counselors should realize that for most of these students, it is a passing adolescent imperfection. In the college recommendation, a broader view should be taken and if **justifiable**, the recommendation should focus on the student's good qualities.

Be Prepared to Write the Recommendation

Whenever juniors come into the counselor's office from January on, take the time to gather relevant information to begin the recommendations early. A sample **College Interview Sheet** is included in **Addendum 6** and asks students such questions as:

1. What is their intended major?
2. At what location do they want to study and at what colleges?
3. What their estimated GPA is? If it is off the mark, the counselor then can supply it as a reality check.
4. What are their in-school activities?
5. What are their significant outside activities or hobbies?
6. What are their significant volunteer activities or social achievements?

7. What honors, AP, IB courses have they taken?

8. What organizations or honor societies do they belong?

In the interview, the skilled counselor should draw as much information as possible from the student. This interview should reveal hidden information that the student may deem inconsequential. **Good probing skills are an asset in this area.** Obtaining this information in the junior year allows the counselor to begin drafting the initial stages of the recommendation when the opportunity arises. In this way, the counselor will not be inundated with five or six recommendations a day when applications begin to pour in during November and December of the following school year. Once the preliminary recommendation is completed, it is a simple matter of updating the recommendation with current information before sending it out.

Case Study

A young woman was applying to a very prestigious university, where it was extremely difficult to gain admittance. At the counselor-student interview session the counselor probed deeply for some unique quality, talent or activity that might be the turning point in the admissions process. The student's grades were commensurate with the acceptance guidelines, but this alone would not be good enough. Seemingly, there was nothing that would differentiate her from the rest of the high-powered students. However, the counselor hit upon the idea of matching the student's high moral values with that of the founding fathers of the university. The counselor was able to state categorically that in the student's application, essays, and personal statements not one word was embellished or enhanced by the candidate to make herself look better than she actually was. Rather than get into the university by a little self-aggrandizement, she stayed with the facts so as to be true herself. Amazingly, she was accepted.

The point here is that the counselor has to be creative in writing a student's recommendation. As much information as possible has to be abstracted from the student. Then, a great deal of thought has to go into the process of presenting the student in the best possible light. Coming up with the idea of a student's personal value system and linking it to the right university takes a great deal of probing, communication and creativity.

Questionable Requests

There are times when a college applicant, whose conduct is questionable, may ask his /her counselor for a recommendation. The college recommendation is part of the student's "educational record" and the student has the right to see these records. If the counselor knows that he/she must be candid with the college, the counselor should request a waiver of the student's rights to read the recommendation. (This release should be a standard practice for all senior students and should be listed on the College Application Cover Page. **Addendum 6**) In the actual recommendation, if the student does not warrant positive comments, the negative need not be indicated. Admissions counselors can read between the lines. One of two things may take place. The counselor may elect to call the admission counselor and fill in the details, or the admissions counselor may phone the counselor and request details. When it comes to the negative, the less that is put in writing, the better. Counselors cannot know every admissions counselor on a personal basis, but the necessity of developing personal contacts is all the more obvious in these cases.

Suspensions

On some college applications there is a question asking if the student has ever been suspended. It is up to the counselor to evaluate exactly what the college means by suspensions. What the colleges are looking for are ways they can protect their student body and avoid any serious campus problems. If the student has been suspended for a very serious problem, which may include severe alcohol abuse, violence, abuse of women, or a serious drug problem including drug distribution, etc., then the college wants to know. Be assured that the counselor will get a follow up call for more information. Failure to notify them will also bring about calls that are more serious and of an accountable nature if the student acts out in a harmful and destructive manner on the college campus.

Notice to Teachers

Junior students are counseled to request college recommendations from their teachers in their junior year, well in advance of sending out their senior applications. A teacher's skill in this area is greatly appreciated and a strong recommendation will make a significant impact on the college acceptance process. Their incisive, specific comments and evaluation are crucial. For the convenience of teachers, the guidance secretaries should type their recommendations.

Late Requests

Many applications are delayed because students fail to provide their teachers with enough advanced notice to write the recommendation. An early alert to a teacher is important since they may have as many as twenty or thirty recommendations to write. This is even more necessary if the teacher is retiring and will not be around the following year. Recommendations that come from outside the school should also be processed early.

Review Teacher Recommendations

Not all teachers possess the art of writing college recommendations. Consequently, the counselor should review all teacher recommendations. If they are too general, lack any real contribution to the student's application, and are poorly written, they should not be included in the application. Without revealing the counselor's evaluation, the counselor should encourage the student to obtain more recommendations. Counselors should never allow students or parents to read teacher recommendations without the express permission of the teacher.

Check the College Name

Counselors should always be sure that if a college is specifically mentioned in a recommendation letter, that it be sent to the correct college. If not, it causes serious problems. There have been cases where the admissions personnel have written back to the sending school's principal with harsh criticism for the counselor in question. This mistake does cause poor college public relations as well. Mistakes of this nature can occur when teachers submit recommendations and mention specific colleges. It is very easy for the counselor just to place teacher recommendations into the college application package without checking if a specific college is mentioned.

Personalizing the College Application

In most cases, the student is merely a name on an application. No one in the college admissions office knows the student personally. As mentioned elsewhere in this handbook, after a college visit is made and the names of the admissions personnel obtained, a thank you letter should be sent. It is also wise for the student to call the college, ask pertinent questions and speak directly to admissions personnel. The student should remind the admissions counselor that he/she has met previously. This procedure applies when meeting admissions reps at college fairs or at a school visit. If there is a connection with the admissions counselor, he or she will recognize the name on the application and read the student's essay and recommendations with more interest.

Requesting Recommendations

When counselors meet with juniors, the counselor should have them indicate the teachers from whom they will be requesting recommendations. Many juniors have not given adequate thought to this important procedure. Having them specify names of these teachers on the spot forces students to make a decision. Direct students to contact teachers early if they expect the recommendation to be finished in time for their college application. This applies even more so to students who are planning to go Early Decision. A request in their junior year is not unreasonable since it gives the teacher more time to write it. It also puts the student's name at the top of the list should the teacher have many recommendations to write.

Preparing for the College Planning Session with Parents and Students

The first step in preparing for the college student-parent session, as previously mentioned, is to interview each junior early in the spring. Take notes on **The College Interview Sheet**, which covers all aspects of the student's academic, athletic, and extra-curricular involvement. It is well to have it done before any parent conference. At the college session, with the parents present, this information allows the counselor to be familiar with the student and his/her college plans. Parents will then feel that the counselor knows their student. Additionally, the counselor will be aware of the student's preferences in colleges and can speak with certainty rather than fielding questions. If the counselor feels confident and he/she has prepared a preliminary draft, the counselor may choose to read the recommendation to the parent. This is a way to praise the student, make the parents feel comfortable with the recommendation and allow the parents to give additional information to be included in the recommendation. Preface the reading of the recommendation by saying that as a school official, you are pleased to read the following. It is unfortunate that parents do not hear their children praised publicly very often. The recommendation presents such an opportunity. If the counselor does not feel comfortable with this procedure, simply proceed with the meeting.

Use of a Quote

When writing student recommendations, it is always well to include a quote from a teacher that knows the intellectual capacity of a student rather than simply stating that the student is bright and incisive in her/his thought process. When the counselor has a high-powered student or a student with special circumstances, the counselor can request from teachers a short quote on a student to be placed in the counselor's recommendation. This may be done on a special form requesting a short paragraph, which would be placed in the recommendation to validate counselor comments. If this procedure is done well in advance, it will be ready for the counselor's final copy.

Recommendations for High-Powered Students

The following may be somewhat controversial, but it has worked to good effect. It is suggested that the counselor put brief marginal comments next to the significant paragraphs in the recommendation. This quickly brings to the attention of the reader the meaning of the paragraph. In a conference with a prominent director of college admissions, he summarized everything about the student on an index card. The above technique becomes a guide for admissions personnel and **emphasizes significant achievements** for their summation. It also allows the counselor to highlight certain thematic areas that the counselor wants to emphasize.

Recommendation Review

A good technique to use, when a prestigious college rep is visiting and the counselor has a high-powered student, is to ask the admissions person to read the counselor's college recommendation for that student. This serves two purposes:

1. It is an opportunity for the counselor to have his/her work critiqued. Be up front with the admissions officer and indicate that you would welcome an evaluation including suggestions for improvement.

2. It is also an opportunity for the admissions officer to get to know the high-powered student you are recommending and another opportunity to talk about that student.

Case Study

Having employed the above technique, the counselor was given some advice on how to improve her letter of recommendation. In addition, the admissions counselor commented that at the previous conference with seniors, the very student who the recommendation was about, knew the most about the college. The point here is that the admissions counselor got to know the student and could put a (favorable) face on the student's application when it was being read. The same technique may be used for a student with special circumstances.

Parental Recommendation

In the course of dealing with parents who really know their kids and can express this special knowledge as no other can, a counselor may suggest that the parent write a recommendation for their son or daughter. This should be a rare occurrence, but one utilized to highlight some special gift, talent or circumstance that can only be best related by a parent.

The Resume

Students should use the resume format recommended by the guidance department. The cardinal point to remember is that admissions personnel are looking for consistent involvement with some level of achievement. Simply to list multiple activities that show no continuous involvement is to take up space and detract from the student's real achievements. Once again, it is well to remember that admissions personnel do not have all day to read a laundry list of multiple pages in small print of activities that go back to grade school. Make the resume easy to read with significant achievements easily identified. A well-organized and properly laid out resume should fit on a single page.

"A good name is worth gold." Proverb
(As said of Olivia)

CHAPTER 20

Financial Aid

(Photo by Paul Caravelli)

The Money Flows like Water...Wasted

Each year millions of dollars are wasted. Parents fail to file the FAFSA (Free Application for Federal Student Aid) on time, fail to explore scholarship opportunities, or think they do not qualify. They become overwhelmed by the filing process, and ignore invitations to attend financial aid nights. The money is there, but the parent has to work to get it. Even some colleges, offering academic scholarships for students without financial need, will require that the FAFSA be filed.

1. The first thing counselors should do is to encourage students and their parents to file the FAFSA as soon as possible after January 1. To wax poetical on the timeliness of filing the FAFSA statement, Shakespeare, using sea imagery, advises parents to be expeditious:

"There is a <u>tide</u> in the affairs of men,
Which, taken at the <u>flood,</u> leads on to <u>fortune,</u> (+$)
Omitted, all the <u>voyage</u> of their life
Is bound in <u>shallows</u> and misery. (-$)
On such a <u>full sea</u> are we now <u>afloat</u>
And we must take the <u>current </u>as it serves,
Or lose the venture." (+$ or -$)
Julius Caesar, Act IV, Sc. 3. **SHAKESPEARE**
(As recommended by Henry Ebbitt)

In other words, file as soon as possible. Using Shakespeare's water analogy, those who take the first swell of the wave, get immediate attention. Those who take the wave at the crest are with the mass of applicants. Those who wait and take the wave as it eddies are the late filers. **Don't procrastinate; colleges have only so much money.**

2. When students decide what college they will attend and have their FASFA results, they should go on the internet and apply for their state's financial aid. In the case of New York students, they should file for the N.Y.S. TAP program. (Each state has its own scholarships and procedures to follow. Check them out).

3. If parents have questions on financial aid, a good technique is to have the parents make an actual appointment with a financial officer at a nearby college. Generally, financial aid officers are very willing to go over the correct way to file the FAFSA. It is good public relations on the part of the college and the parents are dealing at the right level for advice.

4. Parents should not get totally discouraged if their first financial aid package from the college is not sufficient. Counselors should encourage parents to make a direct contact either in person or by phone to one of the college's financial aid officers to explain their economic situation and

their real need. They should be persistent if they want to get results. Likewise, the counselor should make a direct contact. This is especially helpful if the counselor has a working relationship with the financial aid officer.

The actual steps for filing a FAFSA are found in **Addendum 8.**

Anecdotes

On one occasion when a parent went directly to the financial aid officer and begged for more financial aid, he was told there was no more aid available. However, during the course of the conversation, the name of a college administrator was mentioned as a friend and miraculously some more money was found.

On another occasion, a counselor took a young lady with severe financial problems to the financial aid office to advocate for more money. Even the presence of a professional counselor pleading for more money and justifying the need did not produce any results. On leaving the building, the counselor fell down three steps, banged her head, bruised her shin, and burst the burse sack in her elbow. When informed of this, the financial officer made contact with the director of finance. Even though the counselor gave "her blood" for the cause, it was to no avail, financial aid was still denied.

IN PLEADING YOUR CASE FOR FINANCIAL AID, SOMETIMES YOU WIN AND SOMETIMES YOU LOSE. NEVERTHELESS, IT IS WORTH THE EFFORT TO TRY

Financial Aid and Compromise

There are real financial considerations in selecting a college. Some parents limit their child's choice to state colleges because they are the most reasonable financially. However, parents should allow their children to aim for the stars. Their circumstance may warrant an excellent financial package. Even if the package does not cover the full tuition, parents may then be willing to sacrifice in order to give their child what he/she considers the best college. (This is not to say that the state universities are not the best, often times they are.) If it is an unreasonable financial package, at least their student will have the satisfaction of knowing that his/her parents did try and that he/she did get into a great college.

Sometimes LESS is MORE

If a student has a long-range goal to continue education beyond the B.A., it is worthwhile to pay less tuition at a state college rather than a much higher tuition at a private college. The money saved will then be available for the ultimate goal, graduate school.

Fee Waivers

There are guidelines for the use of the fee waiver for college applications. If a student does not meet the criteria but the counselor feels there is justification for the waiver, the counselor should call the college and explain the circumstance or attach a note to the application. Some colleges are very liberal about this arrangement and are glad to get an additional application.

Scholarships

Guidance departments usually publish a list of all scholarships available to students. The sources and criteria may vary. This should be the primary source of information. Other sources may include but are not limited to the following:

1. Individual college academic scholarships
2. Scholarships that relate to a parent's job, military service, union, etc.
3. Scholarships that relate to a certain ethnicity
4. Scholarships that relate to a particular athletic, musical, or artistic talent
5. Scholarships that relate to a handicapping condition
6. Scholarships that relate to volunteer work
7. Scholarships that relate to a particular college major
8. Scholarships that relate to financial need
9. Scholarships that are offered through competitive exams or essays

10. Scholarships offered by large companies, e.g. Coca Cola
11. Etc.

Scholarship Companies

Be leery of companies that charge a fee for a college scholarship search. With extra work on the part of the parent and student, most of the information on scholarships may be obtained on the internet. Scholarship money comes only after extensive research, determination and the effort to fill out the scholarship application. Two **free web sites are:**

1. www.FastWeb.com is the nation's largest source of national and local college scholarships that are worth over $1 billion.
2. www.scholarships.com offers the same free service.

(EOP) Educational Opportunity Program

The Educational Opportunity Program is for students who meet certain financial needs and academic guidelines. The counselors have to be aware of these youngsters in their caseload and advise them of the financial benefits of the EOP. It is advised that a specific review of the counselor's caseload be made to identify these students early on and alert them to the program.

(FSEOG) Federal Supplemental Educational Opportunity Grant

A FSEOG is for undergraduates with exceptional need—that is, students with the lowest EFC, (Effective Family Contributions,) and gives priority to students who receive Federal Pell Grants. An FSEOG does **not have to be paid back.**

The U.S. Department of Education guarantees that each participating college will receive enough money to pay the Federal Pell Grants of its eligible students. There is no guarantee every eligible student will be able to receive an FSEOG; students at each college will be awarded these funds based on availability of funds at that school.

Students can receive between $100 and $4,000 a year, depending on when they apply, meet the funding level of the college and the policies of the financial aid office at the college.

The college will credit the student's account or pay the student directly (usually by check), or combine these methods. College must pay students at least once per term (semester), trimester, or quarter. Generally, colleges that do not use traditional terms must pay the student at least twice during the academic year. (Taken from The Student Guide—Financial Aid from the U.S. Department of Education.)

"Success calls for sacrifice. The life of achievement is a life of hard work." Alfred A. Montapert (As suggested by Jeanmarie and Keira Pombar)

CHAPTER 21

Transcripts

Nomenclature

When reviewing a transferring student's transcript, try to align the nomenclature of the transferring school to your school. If the former school lists the class as World Studies and the curriculum is the same as your Global Studies, list the class as Global Studies. This avoids confusion when it comes to determining graduation requirements. Always make a duplicate copy of the transferring student's transcript. Place the original in the student's cumulative folder and the photocopy in your anecdotal folder for ready reference. It may take weeks before the transcript is complete because the transferring records are incomplete or not forwarded from the transferring school.

It is imperative that all new students have current and updated grades. There are times when a transferring student fails to notify the counselor of summer school grades. Any student who has attended summer school must transfer their grades to the new school.

Missing Grades

When grades are missing on a transcript, the counselor should call the former school. If they indicate that they will send an updated transcript, make a note in the "follow up" file. Keep checking until the grades are received. Sometimes it takes weeks before the grades arrive. Sometimes what is promised is not delivered and there must be an additional follow up call.

Reviewing Transcripts

In reviewing transcripts from a sending school:

1. Check to see if there were any 8th grade courses that were offered for high school credit.

2. When there is any doubt, the counselor has to phone the sending school for clarification.

3. If it involves a grade change, have the school validate the change.

4. When transferring letter grades to numerical grades or "visa versa," make sure that they are exact. A uniform chart prepared by the administration and uniformly followed by all counselors should be in place. This is especially necessary, if it involves a student's GPA and the possibility of the choice of school valedictorian.

Record Transcripts Immediately

Students who transfer in their senior year should have their transcripts recorded immediately. If one of these students is a contender for valedictorian, a school policy should be followed. In most cases, the transferring student if he/she is a senior is usually ranked separately and not eligible for this honor.

Placing Twelfth Grade Transferring Students

Throughout the year, including May and June, students are admitted into school. Placing them in classes can be quite difficult, based upon their educational needs and the courses their former school offered. At times, some flexibility on the part of teachers is required to accommodate these students in the transition. In a notice to teachers, counselors should attach all previous grades for the year and in those cases where science labs were required, the lab reports as well. Sometimes the curriculum course content does not match exactly, which makes it more difficult for the teacher. It is always an easier pill for teachers to swallow if the counselor has a good working relationship with these teachers.

Anecdote

Believe it or not, some parents, in the interest of their child, will request a check of the grades of another student, especially if only a few hundreds of a point separates a student from being valedictorian. In the cases of transferring students' transcripts, they wish to validate grades and courses taken. Counselors will go into the records, check the competing student's transcript, and challenge a grade that might be questionable. Courses that are taken for extra credit, transferred credits, independent study courses, etc. can all be called into question if not clearly validated.

As they say, "a fine kettle of fish" would be brewed if one of the courses was not in fact validated and the counselor has to deal with infuriated parents over their student's GPA.

Review Transcripts

Before finalizing the senior transcripts in late September for distribution during the senior year, a copy of the transcript should be mailed home for parents and students to check and notify the school of any error. Sometimes teachers tell students that they will change a grade and it is not indicated on the transcript.

1. If changes are to be made, notify the secretary in charge of the changes.

2. Keep a list of all seniors who need to pass specific course requirements.

3. Senior transcripts should be checked in the summer of the senior year to make sure that seniors are taking the right courses and meet all the requirements for graduation. Parents should be notified if the student may not be graduating and the courses that are needed. Again, in January, the transcripts should be updated with semester course grades and should be verified so that the students are still candidates for graduation.

Collusion

Regrettably, some parents will back their son or daughter in a lie if it will improve the student's GPA on the final transcript. Thankfully, this is rare. Some of the more common ploys to improve grades are:

1. To claim the teacher lost their child's term paper or report, when in reality it was never handed to the teacher.

2. To skip a test in order to get more time to study

3. To question a teacher's grading methods

4. Some parents are so bold as to try to enlist the aid of the counselor in grade manipulation with some contorted story about the teacher's poor organizational skills. The counselor has to be very careful to contact the teacher in question to find out the true story.

Case Study

It is a rare occasion when a student and parent join to actually change a grade and indicate its validity. However, such an incident occurred as a young woman went to summer school for a failure in science.

The grade on the master list that was sent to the school indicated that the student had failed the science course. Unfortunately, it was somewhat blurred. The counselor placed the student in a repeat course. The student on being placed indicated that she had passed the course and should be in the next level and that she had proof of passing. On the premise that should this be true, the counselor placed the student in the next level of science until the issued was resolved. It is always easier to go back into a repeat subject than to move a student into an advanced subject after it has begun.

Naturally, the student and parent delayed producing their proof in the hope that the issue would go away and the student would remain in the course as a "fait acompli." In the meantime, the counselor was persistent. She called the administrator of the summer school, who in turn called the summer school teacher. It was confirmed as a failure. Upon hearing of this news, the parent insisted he had a letter indicating that his child had passed and would produce it. He did bring it in and the letter did have a passing grade. It was perfect except for one slight miss-alignment. The parent even produced the original envelope. This was easy enough, since it was the original envelope that the failure notification came.

The matter was referred to the principal and he ruled that the student had failed the course based on the information provided by the counselor. Reluctantly, the parent agreed that the student must repeat the course, never admitting a forgery. The student was placed properly after all due process. Ironically, a few days latter when the counselor checked to see if the student had gone to the proper class, she was still playing the game by remaining in the advanced class. She was then chaperoned by the counselor to the right class and the assistant principal was notified.

When dealing with parents who attempt to manipulate grades, they are not beyond deceitfully backing their son or daughter in other areas as well:

1. When their child is truant, the parent will call to claim that the student is absent.

2. They will falsify the need for a schedule change to get a "better" teacher.

3. They will request to drop a course the student is failing late in the school year on some pretext of anxiety or pressure, etc.

TRANSCRIPTS: *"carrier of news and knowledge..."*
Charles W. Eliot (As suggested by David O'Connell, Jr.)

CHAPTER 22

Grade Reporting

A Quick Overview

When the counselor receives student report cards, he/she may not have time to do an extensive review. However, a quick overview, which could only take five minuets to page through, is invaluable. The counselor should make mental notes on good performance or failures. Then when the counselor sees students in the hallway, he/she can compliment or encourage them. If parents call, the counselor has a quick point of reference and is not caught unaware. When the counselor has more time, he/she can make a failure list or ask for a print out of failures and then call failing students to the office for an academic conference.

Incompletes

There will be instances of incompletes on the report cards, generally because students fail to turn in reports or assignments. School registrars issue guidelines each year for the timely delivery of grades. In those cases where an **incomplete** is required, there should be a specific form to change the incomplete grade. In most schools, it is to be delivered to the registrar, not to the guidance counselor. The change of grade form is available in the guidance office. Incompletes are inevitable but unless they are addressed, they turn into failures.

Summer School Grades

When students bring in a copy of their transcripts from summer school or other schools, the counselor must always double check with the sending school for accuracy. The counselor must always work from an official document.

Independent Study

If a teacher is sponsoring an Independent Study Program, an Independent Study application form may be picked up in the Guidance Office. Students must initiate the process and submit the form to the proper personnel for approval. Upon completion of the Independent Study, the teacher must submit a final grade on the proper form to the registrar. The registrar, in turn, should notify the counselor of its completion.

Teacher or Student Requests

Whenever a student or teacher comes to the counselor with a request for a grade change, kindly ask them to fill out the proper form so that it can be submitted to the registrar. If the case needs further investigation, the counselor may assist by noting it in the "follow up folder" as a reminder until the grade is finalized.

Out of District Students

Some students are placed out of district by the C.S.E. (Committee on Special Education), etc. Parents will usually request that their child graduate from the home school and attend the graduation ceremony. To do this, these students must meet the home high school graduation requirements. The counselor also should check the school board policy on this since some of these students could have disciplinary problems. If they are approved, refer the parents to the **"Whom to Contact List"** (**Addendum 3.**) so that information on cap and gowns, pictures, prom, etc. is sent to them. If your school does not have a **"Whom to Contact List,"** refer the parent to the main office secretary. Counselors should be careful not to be caught in the "graduation web." Any failure to place a student in the yearbook or on a graduation list, etc., will be blamed on the counselor if she/he decides to take on the task.

Early Notification of Grades

If students apply to a college for early decision/early action, before the first **semester** report cards are given out and the student has received good grades for the **first quarter** marking period, the grades should be sent to the college. Usually only the **first semester** grades are sent by the home school. The quarter grades become the responsibility of the counselor, if he/she so wishes. A quick way of doing this is to have the student fill out the college addresses on school envelopes while the counselor photocopies the report card.

The student can stuff the envelope(s) under the counselor's supervision and then the counselor mails them with a short cover letter. There is another way of doing this; simply have the secretaries do it. However, the above method is faster and the secretaries appreciate the help at a busy time of the year. If the grades are not good, the counselor is not obliged to send **first quarter** grades. Grades will be sent at the end of the first semester.

Case Study

Each year after the first semester, colleges request the first semester grades. A high-powered student, whether subconsciously or deliberately, did very poorly because of a reaction to excessive parental pressure. She became passive aggressive and purposely did very poorly. She had applied to many academically challenging colleges. Her parents requested that her mid-year grades not be sent unless requested by the college. As it turned out, two colleges requested them, both were very demanding in their acceptance qualifications. The counselor wrote a letter of explanation giving the reasons for her poor performance. The letter explained the mitigating circumstances in detail but did not hold the student blameless. However, the circumstances were explained. One of the two colleges denied her outright; the other gave a guaranteed acceptance after one year at another college. All the other colleges, which did not receive her mid-year grades, in spite of the fact that she had a 94 average and high SAT scores, denied her acceptance. The parents were counting on previous performance to get her through. A better approach would have been to send the first semester grades as poorly as they were, with the letter of explanation.

"Whatever is worth doing at all, is worth doing well"
Lord Chesterfield (As found in the philosophical writings of Professors Eileen and Dan White)

CHAPTER 23

Testing
Test Anxiety

In every school population, there are a number of students, who experience test anxiety beyond what is normal. These students have genuine apprehension. The pity of the situation is that they typically do not share this anxiety with their counselor. Once the counselor has been informed of such a problem, then work can begin to put the student at ease. There are books written on the subject but a basic approach is to reassure the student that the test is manageable. Even the presence of the counselor at the beginning of the test to encourage the student is helpful. A call to the parents, after the exam has begun advising them that all is well to this point, is gratefully received. This team approach between the parents and counselor is necessary to help the youngster gain more confidence in his/her ability to overcome test anxiety.

Memorize It

At the beginning of each year, the counselor should encourage students to review thoroughly the registration booklets for the ACT or SAT to become aware of procedures and directives. Likewise, the counselor should advise students to become aware of registration deadlines. Procedures for changing a test center, special circumstances, stand by testing, fee waivers, etc. should be familiar to them. They should be encouraged to read the registration book, cover to cover.

Code Numbers

Every high school has a school code number and a test center number. For the convenience of parents and students, these numbers should be stamped on the front of the test application booklets.

Testing Accommodations for L.D. or 504 Students

It is imperative at the time of a student's CSE special education classification or 504 designation, that whoever is responsible for filing the SSD accommodation form, do so immediately. The parents are present at these meetings and the opportunity to have them sign the form is opportune.

SAT or ACT

When deciding whether to put a SAT or ACT score on the college application, there is a chart supplied by the ACT organization, which converts the ACT to SAT scores and *visa versa*. Select and send the higher scores of the two tests. Most colleges request that whatever score you send that it comes directly form that organization.

SAT II Testing

It is most helpful to students and counselors if teachers remind their students to register for upcoming exams, especially the SAT II tests. The information on applying for these exams is readily available in the guidance office. These exams are best taken in June when students are most ready and have just completed the coursework covered on the subject test. Students in grades 9 or 10 who are taking a specialized course that qualifies for an SAT II exam should be encouraged to take the test in June, since the knowledge for the exam is proximate.

Which Should I Take

The choice to take the ACT or SAT I, really comes down to the individual. Generally, the ACT covers more material in history and science, as well as math and English content. It also has a summative score. If the student feels that he/she has a broader type knowledge, then he/she may choose the ACT. Many students, who can afford it, take review courses. If this is the case then the type preparation the student receives in the review course will determine which to take. Once again, if the student can afford to take the review course or the school offers a free one, **it is highly recommended that students take these review courses.** The advantage of the review course is that the student not only gains more knowledge but also becomes test wise. Techniques, procedures, and hints are provided on how to recognize and answer certain questions, as well as the efficient use of time.

If the school does not offer a review course, then a concerted effort by the PTA should be made to convince the Board of Education to offer one. Lack of such a course puts financially poorer students at another disadvantage.

Poor SAT Scores

There are good students who score poorly on the SAT/ACT's and because of this could be jeopardized in the college admissions process. There is some **hope** for these students in that there are colleges, which do not consider the SAT/ACT scores. They are listed on the internet as **www.fairtest.org/optsat.htm** This list includes colleges and universities that do not use the SAT I or ACT to make admissions decisions. Some colleges exempt students who meet grade point averages or class rank criteria. Others require SAT or ACT scores but use them only for placement purposes or to conduct research studies. Check with the college's admissions office you are interested in to learn more about specific admissions requirements.

Taking Advanced Placement and Honors Courses

If students have the option of self-selecting AP courses or honors courses and the counselor feels the selection is inappropriate, please confer with the student and the parent. To re-enforce your point, teacher assessments should also be utilized. Should the student elect to take the course, it is permitted within the guidelines of the "self-select" process but the counselor's assessment will remain on record. (The self-selection choice applies when schools allow the student the option of taking an AP course.)

AP Exams for Students Not in AP Courses

If a student is very well read and informed on the content of an AP course but does not qualify for acceptance into the AP course, the counselor should check to see if the school will allow the student to sign up for an AP exam in a content area. If not, the counselor should call around to other schools. Some of these students score very well on AP's and it will enhance their academic record.

"The man, who makes no mistakes, does not usually make anything." Marcus Cato (As recommended by Dotti and Ed Durrschmidt)

CHAPTER 24

Telephone Calls

Take Calls

I n the best of all words, counselors should never interrupt a counseling
session by taking a phone call. However, with the multiple demands
placed on counselors and with caseloads, which could be in the
hundreds, some exceptions apply to get the job done.

The following advice may be controversial but it is a technique,
which, if used properly, can be of great advantage to the counselor. If
possible (even though when involved with a student), take all incoming
calls from parents. Most student conversations are not of a grave nature
and can be interrupted to take a brief phone call. First, ask the student
if he/she would not mind if you take a call. This is a courtesy, which

students appreciate. If it interrupts an important counseling session, ask the secretary to take a detailed message and say the counselor is with a student and will back to them.

This procedure may seem strange but the advantage is that the counselor gets the reputation for a rapid response. The counselor also saves time by avoiding follow-up phone calls. If the call requires extended time, tell the party that you will get back. Be sure to mention that you are with a student. This will shorten the conversation and will be a message to the public that you are involved with students but place a high priority on facilitating parental concerns. A procedure has to be set in place with the guidance secretary. It is very simple to instruct the secretary that she should intercom the counselor indicting who is on the phone. Then the counselor can make the decision to receive the call. Many times the counselor has been trying to get the party and it would be a grave inconvenience not to receive the call. If the counselor has to call back there is also the possibility of missing the parent and the necessity of making still another call.

Avoid the reputation that, "The counselor never returns my calls." When complaining about the counselor, from whom they wish to detach themselves, they will not say "My Counselor."

Our Best Ally or Worst Enemy

The telephone can be the counselor's best ally or worst enemy. Learn to use it to your best advantage. There is nothing a parent appreciates more than to receive a call from the counselor offering help, concern, and advice. Even if the reason might be to share bad news, it is still appreciated. The phone is an especially useful tool if the student is sick, has achieved something significant, is discouraged, etc. When sick or having accomplished something significant, the student is delighted to receive a phone call from his/her counselor. In a sense, the telephone can be used as a tool to bond wherein the student becomes a loyal friend of the counselor.

Frequent Parental Calls

Each year the counselor will have a handful of parents who demand a great deal of time with frequent calls and meetings. There are two ways of handling them. Negatively, you can be curt and explain that you do not have the luxury of a great deal of time to speak with them. This may have some effect, but will not satisfy them and chances are you will likely alienate these parents. If they are the demanding type, they will bad mouth the counselor in the community and to the administration. Positively, the preferred strategy is to answer their calls explaining that you are with a student or in the middle of a meeting or dealing with an emergency. As a courtesy, you are taking the call but must be brief. In this way, these parents will understand how busy you are and will appreciate that you took time to respond to them, if only briefly. In addition, instead of badmouthing the counselor, they will more likely praise you in the community.

Phone Memo Messages

Whenever the counselor receives a phone memo, always save the message and if possible make some notations on the memo. This will validate that you returned the phone call and had subsequent follow-up. The memo is usually dated and, if needed, contains the party's phone number for future reference. They need not be filed separately, but saved in a place set aside just for telephone memos.

Out to Lunch

When the counselor is unavailable to take a call, secretaries should be instructed on how to respond to a parent. Secretaries should not say the counselor is unavailable or the counselor is taking a break or is at lunch. A better response that covers all bases is that the counselor is in a meeting or has left for a meeting and will get back to the caller. This is more professional and guards against the misconception that the counselor is never in the office or off on trivial matters.

Who Said What

There are times when parents will call to question information or advice the counselor has given their son or daughter. Some students are manipulative and change information to their advantage. When this happens, it is best to have a parent conference with both the student and parent in attendance to clarify the issue.

A Teacher's Phone Number

As a matter of policy, counselors can never give out a teacher's home phone number to students, parents or other third parties unless instructed to do so by the teacher.

Telephone Advice

Make it a priority to return all calls the same day they are received. It will save the counselor from getting, again, a poor reputation. "**The counselor never returns my calls.**" Returning calls can be difficult during a very busy day and especially if an evening meeting is to follow. If a call cannot be made, have your secretary call the parents and indicate that you will be attending a night meeting and you will get back the very next day.

Confirmation

When calling parents at home concerning problematic students, the students themselves may intercept the counselor's phone messages left on the family answering machine and delete them. Be sure to indicate in the message that you want confirmation by a returned phone call and that your message was received. In your file, note the date and time of the call. In this way, the counselor is covered and if the student does intercept the message, he/she is under pressure not to erase it. If there is no response, a certified letter should be sent with a return receipt.

"It is a luxury to be understood." Ralph Waldo Emerson
(As suggested by Dr. Maureen Larkin)

CHAPTER 25

Guidance Passes

Contacting Students

Each school system has its method of contacting students to come to the guidance office to meet with the counselor. Some schools use the intercom system. The most prevalent is the use of the guidance pass. The first step in the delivery of guidance passes is that of teacher cooperation. Passes cannot be delivered if left in the teacher's mailbox. Teachers forget or get into the habit of not going to their mailbox to obtain them. This is a crucial area for teacher cooperation. If a consistent pattern of neglect occurs regarding the failure to deliver guidance passes, a friendly conversation with the teacher is in order. Explain to the teacher that the effectiveness of the counselor's work begins with the student coming to the counselor's office. Part of this teacher conference should include the concept that instruction is the primary concern of the teacher and the counselor understands this. In the overview, however, there are times when a meeting with the student and the counselor is necessary and may necessitate loss of class time.

If the school uses an intercom system to call students to the counselor's office, in one sense it is more effective than a pass. The drawback, aside from possibly embarrassing the student, is that the call may interrupt a teacher's lesson. Since teaching is the primary function of the school, teachers regard their classroom as sacrosanct and any interruption is viewed as a major distraction. Some counselors pause to listen before speaking over the public address system to gage if the interruption will seriously disrupt the class. Failure to respect the teacher's lesson, unless there is an emergency, will cause hard feelings and may affect future counselor-teacher relations.

Where Are the Students?"

Each morning counselors issue guidance passes requesting that students come to the Guidance Office. Therefore, distributing these passes to students is most important. Often times, counselors need to discuss urgent and critical matters with a student. The simple process of delivering a guidance pass may be far more important than it seems. Staff should be made aware of this. One of the most exasperating parts of the counselor's day is that students do not show up. It is most helpful to the teacher if the pass contains a check-off list of the reasons for the meeting. Simple messages indicating the nature of the appointment may be checked off on the pass:

1. Scheduling
2. College Conference
3. Academic conference
4. Follow up
5. Important!
6. Confidential
7. Parental meeting

If the pass has to be returned because the student is unavailable, the reason for the return should be indicated on the pass. The guidance counselor can then make an alternate plan. On the pass, a checklist of the reasons why the student cannot come should be listed:

1. Absent
2. Testing
3. Field trip
4. Involved in a class project
5. Other____

When the pass is returned, it signals the counselors not to waste time waiting for the student.

For additional information on Guidance Passes, **see Chapter 2, Guidance and Students.**

"Diligence is the mother of good fortune." Cervantes
(As researched by Mabel and Bob McNamee)

CHAPTER 26

Record Keeping

Keep Good Records

Many times administrators will ask for reports that go back a few years. Keep good records, especially of cases in which the counselor has done extensive research. Save all old report cards, progress reports, grade sheets, counselor copies of SAT and ACT scores, and SSD records for at least two years. Many times official records do not reflect what the counselor has in her/his records due to entry failures. Always keep a draw for "throwaways." These items may no longer be of use but are, at times, referred to at a later date. Such items would include: administrative notices, schedules, calendar of events, phone messages, etc. Do not become a pack rat but at the same time keep these items for an extended period. Save them but discard them in a timely fashion. One advantage of a binder system is that the binder can be saved and referred to a few years later.

Student Record Keeping

It is recommended that when a student exhibits instances of a disciplinary nature, academic deficiencies or anti-social behavior that a log be kept. This anecdotal information is extremely helpful in parent meetings and provides added validity to teacher and counselor comments.

Summer School

Save all summer school records for at least two years. Be sure to double check the student's schedule to make sure he/she is in the right classes, especially if the student fails in summer school.

Cumulative Folder

When reviewing the confidential cumulative folder, never delete anything, even scraps of paper that seem inconsequential.

Safe Guard Folders

Whenever the counselor takes a folder out of the official file, make sure to return it immediately. If not, keep it in your desk; inform the secretaries where it is, and **lock it in** your desk. <u>Never</u> take the official file home. Loss of official records is not only very serious but also at times irreplaceable and subjects the counselor to extreme accountability.

See the Chapter 15 on "Confidentiality" for more details on record keeping.

"…where no plan is laid…..chaos will soon reign." Unknown
(As quoted in his thesis "On Social Order" by Dr. Gregory Reisert)

CHAPTER 27

Schedule Changes

How to Handle a Difficult Teacher Change

Most schools do not allow counselors to change teachers. When students come to see the counselor and the counselor knows that the answer is "NO," say it cannot be done. If you review the schedule privately, it may reveal that it is not even physically possible to make the requested change. If this is the case and the counselor shares the information, the student will feel that the counselor at least made an effort and, then, it is the student's decision to remain with that teacher. This method also allows the student to see that the counselor is concerned and trying to help. It is also well to recommend a source of tutoring if the student is failing.

Scheduling Time Bombs

A schedule change can easily become a time bomb for counselors. There are so many aspects in the process to consider. Any one mistake can bring parents, administrators, teachers or students, irate and complaining back to the counselor's door. Any mistake in any one of the following areas will likely offend someone:

1. Class size
2. Principal's special directives
3. Pre-requisites
4. Not following schedule change polices
5. Not using the "Schedule Request Form," or a similar form
6. Placing a student in a class that the student does not qualify for academically

7. Placing a student in a class for which the student is over qualified

8. Placing a student in the wrong grade level

9. Placing a student in a class with the same teacher that the student failed the year previously

10. Failing to check the "Follow up List" which indicates courses that students need to graduate

11. Failing to use preventative scheduling if a teacher and student are incompatible

12. Failing to assign the requisite number of courses required by school policy

13. Placing a student in a class that has progressed beyond the point where the student can catch up.

Any one of these mistakes can easily be made, especially at the opening of school when the counselor is bombarded by requests. Pressure is on the counselor to get the school open with as few changes as possible. Additional pressure is added when department heads, teachers and administrators complain at the numerous changes the counselor is making.

Preventative Measures

The counselor can obviate many mistakes in the formative stages of programming schedules for the coming year. The following are offered for consideration:

At the beginning of the scheduling session, list all **required** courses on a piece of paper or on the blackboard, which students must take for their grade level. The school should supply a course description booklet to students to facilitate this process.

2. If a teacher or departmental approval is required for a course, the counselor should be sure to have a list of students who qualify. This is the responsibility of the guidance department head to coordinate this information with other department heads. This should be done well in advance, and should be in place before scheduling begins. In compiling

this list, some teachers are uncertain if a student should be recommended. They prefer to wait until the end of the year. This makes the student apprehensive and the counselor concerned about rearranging a student's schedule at the end of the year, which is more difficult. In this case, teachers who move a student up at the end of the year are obliged to inform the student of the decision. A written note should be sent to the counselor to verify the change and not simply to request that the student notify the counselor.

3. It is the responsibility of each department to notify parents of level changes, especially a level change down. If there are any objections, they should be worked out before the list is submitted to the guidance department. As previously noted, the teacher making the recommendations knows the reasons and should inform the parent of the reason for the change.

4. Have your "Follow up List" available to advise students of courses to be make up.

5. Review electives and their pre-requisites. Prior to actual scheduling, all departments should make presentations to their students on the content and nature of all electives. Departments that fail to do this, do a real disservice to themselves. Many wonderful electives are dropped from the curriculum because students do not fully understand their content and do not sign up for them.

6. When a student is finished filling out the schedule for the coming year, if done in a group session, have the student exchange the proposed schedule with a classmate to review it for completeness.

7. The counselor should **then double check** each schedule individually for the required courses to be taken and to assure that the requisite number of courses is listed.

8. The counselor should insist that every schedule be taken home for parental approval and that it is signed off as acceptable. The approved schedule form should be returned and filed.

9. For change requests to the schedule that are acceptable, make the changes and save the paper work.

10. In cases of severe student-teacher conflicts, a review should be made of each of these students' schedule to obviate future difficulties. When necessary, a parent conference should be held before school opens to make sure all social conflicts and problematic issues are avoided.

11. For a special education student who may have a conflict in the schedule or the student is misplaced, additional private sessions with parents should be held before school opens.

12. When dealing with parents who have serious concerns about their son or daughter's schedule for the coming year, direct them to call for an appointment before school opens to clear up any problems. This may not be feasible for schools that do not provide a counselor before the opening of school. (Any problem that may be obviated before school opens will save the counselor an immense amount of **time and angst.**)

Advising a Parent on a Teacher Change

Occasionally, counselors receive letters from parents demanding a change of teacher. At this time, the school policy should be explained. Then, it is well before the counselor does anything, to obtain the teacher's side of the story. Sometimes a simple phone call from the teacher to the parent can resolve the problem. However, there are exceptions. If the counselor agrees with the parent that a teacher change should be made, a great deal of preparation should be made before going to the department head or the principal. The counselor must decide if he/she should accompany the parent. The parent should be prepared to present a strong case with the reasons for the change.

Process

In the matter of schedule changes, especially concerning the dropping of honors level courses, or AP and IB courses, the counselor should always be sure to process the change according to school policy. Communication with department heads, teachers, and parents is necessary before approval can be given. There are some cases where even the input of the principal is necessary. This will ensure that the chain of command approves the change. Never assume that there are no obstacles in the way and that the counselor can make the change without due process. In many cases, there is a hidden agenda, such as class size. In the case of IB courses, dropping an upper level course may deprive the student of an IB diploma. Approval for this change should be discussed with the parent, department head or IB coordinator before taking action.

Document Negative Changes

Some parents will push to drop a subject due to lack of confidence in a teacher or for fear that the subject matter is too difficult and it will affect the student's grade point average. In these cases, explain to the parent that the extra effort required to succeed may provide the student with intellectual and organizational skills that will serve him/her well in college and add substance to the transcript. College admissions personnel look favorably upon honors level courses. If the parent insists and the change is within school guidelines, the counselor should have the parents sign a statement to the effect that they realize the student's moving down a level may have some bearing on the college application decision.

Which is Better?

Which is better, staying in an honors level course with poor grades, or switching to a lower level course and getting higher grades? The answer is that it is all a matter of degree. If the grades in the honors level course are poor and a genuine effort has been made, then switch. If the grades are in the eighties, then the designation of an honors level course has two advantages. Honors level courses usually carry more weight in calculating the over all grade point average. They are also looked upon more favorably by the colleges because they are more challenging and reflect a higher achieving student.

What a Can of Worms!

The counselor should always check on class size before making a change. Not to do so will result in an overload. An irate teacher will report this immediately to his /her department head, who will, in turn, be down to see the director of guidance. The change will be voided and the counselor embarrassed, if not reprimanded. The counselor will have to redo the schedule. When the schedule is reverted to the original, then the parents will be up in arms demanding the change be kept in place. What a can of worms! Now the counselor has to explain that the change cannot take place because of class size. But the parent will say, "How does one more student make a difference?" And on, and on.... Better first to check to see if there are other sections of the course open with fewer students.

Missing Subjects

If a student is missing a subject, well into the school year because of the counselor's oversight, it is best to handle it discreetly with the receiving teacher before having the student admitted to the class. After explaining the problem to the teacher, make the placement even though you might be embarrassed. You will be held accountable none-the-less. The student is also accountable for not reporting a missing course, but the blame usually reverts in high school to the counselor. The less people involved the better. Once again, a good working relationship with teachers is invaluable.

(Why is it that in college a student who fails to take a required course is at fault....not the counselor? What message is being sent to the high school student when the blame is placed on the counselor?)

A Student's Word

Never take a student's word that a teacher or parent has agreed to a schedule change. Get it in writing and always double check with the people involved.

Consistency and Schedule Changes

If the counselor denies a schedule change for one student based on policy, the counselor must follow that protocol for all students making similar requests. Do not get trapped by inconsistency, "You did it for her/him, but not for me." This also applies to other counselors. If one is lax and the other follows school policy, there is inconsistency within the department causing undue pressure on the counselor following school regulations.

Anxiety and Depression

There are times when the counselor will be puzzled regarding a student's request for a schedule change. For example, is the student requesting a schedule change because he/she is manipulative or truly anxious or depressed? Always proceed in favor of the student. Before making the change, however, investigate the cause of the behavior with the teacher, school psychologist, and parents, etc.

Chronic Schedule Changers

Some students are very social and will maneuver to change their schedules to be with their friends. Recognize this early and nip it in the bud. If not nipped in the bud, it will become a weekly event, repeated each year.

Use of "A Request for Schedule Change Form" by Students

If a student would like to change a class, the "Request for Schedule Change" form (or something similar) must be filled out, signed by the teacher, the department head, the parent, and the counselor.

Avoiding Problems

Every school has its policy on schedule changes, which must be adhered to steadfastly. However, there are windows of opportunity when schedule changes may be made without repercussions. These are during the summer, at the very beginning of the year or at the semester change where there may be course conflicts, level changes or counselor mistakes. Staff usually expects changes at these times. If a student comes to the counselor, with a request for a teacher change because of a personality conflict, and it is valid, make it. If a student wants lunch at a different time for medical reasons, etc., do it. Always try to justify a change by the necessity of arranging the student's schedule. If a student wants to drop an elective, or take an elective, etc., do it, so long as the student has the school-required number of courses. When reviewing schedules during the summer, if the counselor sees a student who is a potential disciplinary problem placed in a weak teacher's class, make the change both for the good of the teacher and the student. In all cases, follow school policy regarding changes. When you can be creative and within school norms, do so. It will save everybody involved a good deal of time and trouble. **A happy student** is a contented student who is more likely to succeed and less likely to seek additional changes as the year progresses.

Blended Classes

As a matter of course, counselors should meet with the director of special education to review the composition of blended classes that contain special education students and mainstream students, as well as another teacher or aide. The composition of this group is important for the success of the group. If there is the possibility of student conflicts or personality clashes, a change should be made before school opens. Once the school year has started, it is very difficult to make changes. From the counselor's point of view, "an ounce of prevention is worth a pound of cure," besides teachers are not happy to receive other teachers' problem students mid-way into the school year.

"There is nothing permanent, except change." Heraclites
(As researched by Eileen O'Brien)

CHAPTER 28

Career Planning

Reinventing the Wheel

There have been many courses given and books written on the topic of careers. And it is not the intent of this handbook to reinvent the wheel. It is significant that towards the end of this handbook, there is the opportunity to re-emphasize the value of having a good working relationship with staff when it comes to career exploration. The areas of technologies, art, drama, dance and music programs are out in the open and their product is easily seen and heard. The counselor should take the opportunity to visit these programs and express an interest in what is going on. In terms of career exploration, the value of these programs to many students is incomparable. Students eagerly look forward to their art, music, drama, and technology courses and they present, for some, an opportunity for excellence. Both students and teachers appreciate someone who will stop in and show an interest. It is another way of keeping in contact with students and learning more about their special talents. Always seek advance permission from the teacher to visit the class while it is in session. This procedure breaks the ice for the counselor and indicates to the teacher that the counselor is interested in the curriculum, wants to learn more about what is going on for future placement, and enjoys seeing the work of his/her students.

Stepchildren of the Curriculum

Teachers in the areas of technology, art, drama, dance, and music often feel their courses are the stepchildren of the curriculum. Some of these teachers feel that no one in the guidance department takes a real interest in the arts. In their mind, the counselors are concentrating on making sure that students meet state requirements and take challenging courses for college preparation. Once a counselor shows a friendly interest in promoting these courses, the pay back is enormous. These courses more easily find a way into students' schedules when they drop a course and need to take another. There will be many times when the counselor will have to go to these teachers for special accommodations and, once again, a good working relationship will greatly facilitate matters.

Technology, Art, Music, Drama and Dance Courses

The importance of these courses for even the brightest of students cannot be stressed sufficiently:

1. For students under academic pressure, these courses give them a break in the day wherein they can do something they like in a relaxed setting and are not subject to extreme pressure.

2. These courses are most beneficial to students who have a keen interest in specialized technologies, etc. or may possess a hidden talent.

3. For weaker students and ELL students such courses situate them in a place where they can excel and be equal, if not superior, to their peers. For them, this may not be possible in other classes.

4. Technology, etc. courses will give some students a very significant introduction to a career path.

Anecdote

One student, known for his misconduct, numerous suspensions, and inability to get along with teachers, was placed in auto shop. There he found an innate skill and, more importantly, began a relationship with the auto tech teacher. When the young man was given the principal's car to work on, he did a superb job. The principal in the interest of his car visited the auto shop and to his amazement found his "favorite" student working on his car. Naturally, a conversation was struck up and the young man was engaged as person with special technical skills. In a sense, they were speaking as equals. This was one of the first times the young man felt good about himself in school. His new relationship with the principal, and the respected guidance of the technology teacher, combined to turn this young man's problems into a success story.

School to Work Programs

Any student wishing to be enrolled in the School to Work program must first see the School to Work Coordinator, and obtain written permission. This program is great for career exploration and an opportunity to lighten up a schedule. It is especially valuable for students who are "at risk" since they will be gainfully employed and have additional contact with a caring coordinator.

Working Papers

Working papers are generally obtained through the nurse's office. Schools may have other ways of processing working papers and a good school "**Whom to Contact List**" should **include this information. (Addendum 3.)**

(BOCES) Board of Cooperative Educational Services

BOCES is an acronym that New York State uses for its career and occupational training centers. For many students it is their pathway to a future career or occupation. The counselor has to be objective in the assessment of students who can truly benefit from this training. If it is costly, counselors may have some reservations because of budgetary pressure. Whatever the cause for holding back, the realization that it might be the academic salvation of "turned off" students, should be the counselor's first concern.

BOCES and ELL Students

BOCES's career programs for ELL students are wonderful opportunities, which can open up an entire career path to a student. Many BOCES programs also provide bi-lingual programs, which facilitate the training of ELL students. There is one danger in the placement of ELL students in BOCES programs. The regular high school diploma must be given first priority if the ELL student has the capability to attain one. This is not to say that ELL students who attend BOCES cannot go on to college. However, the academic training at the home school is a better preparation for completing a college degree. If an ELL student wants specifically to pursue a trade at a technical college, then the training at BOCES is most suitable. Likewise, if an ELL student, knowing that he/she will age out by 21, wants to follow a career path over completing the high school diploma, the counselor must make every effort to place the student in a BOCES program.

(ASVAB) Armed Services Vocational Aptitude Battery

Each high school has the opportunity to offer the ASVAB through the military. Again, follow the directives of school policy. In a manner similar to college reps., the military may be invited to set up a table and explain the nature and benefits of the ASVAB. Generally, this vocational battery is given only to juniors and seniors.

Interest Inventories

One of the most important surveys, as well as a time consumer, is the interest inventory wherein students answer questions, which reveal possible career paths based on particular interests. Parents see the necessity of this information in planning for their student's future. It is also very helpful in assisting students to choose a college major. Its value is commensurate with the effort required to administer it. However, visit the website **www.CollegeBoard.com** for a free interest inventory that is self-administered and scored. The counselor can advise the student to take it and return later to discuss the results. There are other inventories and each school may have a program that they administer to various grade levels. If so, one should take full advantage of it.

The "WISE" Program

The Wise Program or other similar names apply to those high schools that offer internships in the second half of the senior year. Such programs are excellent opportunities for seniors to explore careers that they think they may be interested in at some future date. Many seniors know what their college major is, but are uncertain as to what career field they will enter. The opportunity to work with professionals and be accountable for various aspects of the job is a real career learning experience.

"The direction in which education starts a man will determine his future life." Plato
(As suggested by Christina and Heather Coyne)

CHAPTER 29

Miscellaneous Topics

Drugs, Alcohol, Suicide, and Psychological Disorders

Guidance services cover a wide range of topics, and even in a handbook such as this, not all of them may be neatly categorized, hence the need for Miscellaneous Topics. Each school has its own policy regarding the above topics. It is imperative to become thoroughly familiar with your school's policy. Don't wait until you are in the middle of a crisis. As a counselor, do not take on the full responsibility of each of these issues. Each must be acted on and is best accomplished through a team effort. If the counselor works with a Pupil Personnel Study Team and has a period of time before he/she must act, share your concerns with other professionals, and get their advice. In this way, the counselor is on record as having acted. Additionally, the counselor will probably get valuable additional help in solving the problem.

Suicide

This topic has been treated elsewhere in the handbook. Once a counselor has experienced the suicide of one of his/her students, no opportunity to reiterate preventative procedures can be passed up. If a student gives any indication of suicidal tendencies, an immediate contact should be made with the school psychologist for assessment. From there, the school protocol should be followed. Do not rely on your assessment alone. Better to be cautious than sorry. There are many indicators of suicidal tendencies and a list can generally be obtained from the school social worker or school psychologist.

Anecdote

Take Nothing for Granted

A counselor in dealing with a young girl, whom the counselor knew as mature and sensible, did not take the girl's indications of suicide seriously. In time, the young girl did commit suicide. She recorded everything in her diary, even the fact that she had mentioned it to her counselor. In a court proceeding initiated by her parents, the counselor was found guilty of neglect of duty. It was unfortunate for the counselor, who everybody considered a good person, but even more tragic was the loss of life that occurred.

Professional Insurance

Every counselor should sign up for professional insurance. No matter how good and honorable their intentions, counselors are still fallible and they can be sued. Having insurance provides peace of mind to the counselor as well as more confidence to act freely on behalf of students.

IB and AP Courses

In the matter of IB (International Baccalaureate) vs. AP. courses, students going for the full IB diploma must complete all IB requirements. They take precedence over any AP course. Where there is room on the schedule and the student can fit in an AP course, do so cautiously. The IB program is very demanding and students could easily stress themselves out by trying to do too much. Students who are taking **standard level courses** and only going for a **certificate** in the IB program may take **AP** courses or **IB higher-level** courses. Most colleges do not accept **standard level** courses for college credit, whereas they do accept **AP** and **IB higher-level** courses. (**Addendum 7.**)

IB and College Awareness

Unfortunately, not all college admissions personnel are aware of the IB program. Some are new admissions personnel and have not been trained to its value in the college admissions process. In this case, the counselor should call the college and discuss the IB program with the director of admissions. Most directors of admissions are familiar with the IB program. They, in turn, should inform the admissions counselor of the college's position regarding the IB program. Some colleges have an admissions person solely in charge of the IB applicants.

E-mail

Counselors who utilize the e-mail system should:

1. Save printed copies of e-mails sent and received each day, if they relate to students. They should be placed in student folders for future reference. Relying on searching your e-mail files can be time-consuming and less than efficient if you need the information right away.

2. Keep in contact with the principal, the director of guidance and significant administrative personnel to update them on issues of mutual concern. E-mail is quick and allows the counselor to contact a large number of people with little effort. However, never let e-mail become the main vehicle of contact with teachers and parents. Nothing replaces personal contact and nothing is more important for counselors than to maintain good staff and parental relations.

3. Some parents abuse e-mail by frequently contacting the counselor and putting demands on him/her, hiding behind the impersonal nature that this mode of communication offers. Many of the techniques indicated in Chapter 24, **Telephone Calls,** apply here to solve the dilemma.

4. Use e-mail to keep teachers up to date on the needs and problems of their students.

(CPS) Child Protective Service

If the counselor **suspects** a child, who is under the age of 18, is being physically, sexually or emotionally abused, or neglected, the counselor is mandated to call CPS. The counselor needs only to have indications of abuse. There is no need to provide any proof. In some schools, the social worker is the person to make the call. Follow school procedures and make sure the call is made.

Room Usage

If a counselor schedules a meeting in a room, or any location, other than his/her office, remember to get clearance for the room. Nothing is more embarrassing than to have a meeting with a parent or group of students and then be told to relocate. To where? This also applies to any after school event that utilizes facilities on school property.

Keys

Counselors should never give their keys to a student for any purpose. They run the risk of having them lost, stolen or duplicated. Stolen items from the school building may be traced back to the lost keys and the counselor rightly held accountable. Never leave a handbag or valuable possessions in your unlocked office where they can be stolen.

Alumni

An aspect of the counselors' work that is not factored into their caseload is the assistance they provide alumni. During their high school years, wonderful relationships are established with students. These students will find it quite natural to call upon counselors after they graduate for help with personal problems and clerical assistance. Counselors have to be on guard not to overburden themselves or to allow themselves to be distracted from their main charge, the present student body.

"In giving advice, seek to help, not please." Solon
(As submitted by Katie Danieli)

EPILOGUE

The Psychology of Change

Or

How to Use This Handbook

An aversion to change is part of the human condition. Changing the prevalent view of the nature of School Guidance Services and counselors is **an uphill battle**. Parents are entrenched in their opinions of the guidance department. Some administrators are unfamiliar with the intricacies of guidance services. Counselors have their own style and manner in which they carry out their responsibilities and are reluctant to change. Teachers feel that they have the inside tract in dealing with students since they spend far more time with them than anyone else in the school system. Guidance secretaries feel they have their ear closest to the voice of the community since they have direct contact with parents through the complaints, special requests, and demands that come through the telephone.

The question is,

"How do you bring about change in Guidance Services when the School Community has **differing and set perceptions** of what guidance counselors should do or not do?

There have been many approaches:

1. Evaluative teams representing statewide and national organizations have been invited to analyze guidance services. They typically leave behind a list of positive attributes and a list of changes they feel will benefit the guidance department. When they re-convene ten years later, little or nothing has changed and they end up making the same recommendations. What has happens in the mean time? Nothing! The

positive elements are still there; the recommendations for change have been acquiesced to, and then ignored. In some ways, effective change in the classroom is easier. The classroom is more visible and open to supervision. However, the inner workings of a counselor are more private, especially behind a closed door.

2. There is another method to bring about change in guidance and that is to bring in a "hot shot" consultant. He or she will meet with staff and various members of the school community, and recommend changes. The difficulty with this approach is that the expert first meets with school administrators and receives directives for change. They may even single out certain counselors. Immediately, the counselors become defensive at the notion that the consultant has been "advised." Most assuredly, the expert will have recommendations for change. The administration may then mandate these changes. If so, a number of things will happen. The changes will be implemented…..for while. Counselors will be resentful because they have not internalized the mandated changes. Once counselors close their doors, they are in their own space and will proceed in the same old way. Additionally, unless the rest of the school community is on board with the recommended changes in the guidance department, there is not a sense of collegiality or of a community spirit working together with counselors as a unit. The counselor alone cannot effect all changes.

3. A third method is the direct approach taken by an administrator. This is usually employed with a counselor who is clearly neglecting his/her duties: arriving to school late, seeing few students, careless about details, caustic with students and parents, wasting time on personal matters, not current with guidance services, etc. Theses failures are not up for dialogue; they must be addressed directly, one on one. Change will definitely take place, but it will be with a resentful attitude and not in a spirit of cooperation.

Again, the question is,
"How do you bring about change in Guidance Services when the School Community has **differing and set perceptions** of what guidance counselors should do or not do?

The answer is meaningful dialogue, which is **objective, collegial, and positive.** It is opposed to the kind of adversarial and counterproductive dialogue that sets counselor opinions against those of administrators or teachers. Subjectively, no matter what others may say, each counselor holds firm to his/her values. Beneath the surface, there is the hidden fear of change and the cost it will involve, negating even useful advice.

However, when good counselors need only to implement subtle changes (improving counseling skills, organizational skills, interpersonal skill, etc.) or simply improving on what they are presently doing, this is a matter for discussion. **By objectively discussing** techniques, concepts, or chapters from this handbook, new and varied approaches may be recognized as valuable and even adopted and, most importantly, **internalized.**

The ideas of a third party outsider are easier to dissect, criticize and even argue over since each individual feels less threatened. When issues are discussed that are not the opinions of anyone in the group, the group tends to be more objective, collegial and positive. The individuals in the group are more open to weighing each other's opinions and, consequently, more likely to accept something that will be a change. A change that will benefit not hurt the individual. Again, the ideas of the third party that can be dissected, criticized, and even fought over do away with the conception that the individuals in the group are on the line or that they are the very ones being evaluated.

And again, the question is, "How do you bring about change in Guidance Services when the School Community has **differing and set perceptions** of what guidance counselors should do or not do?

The answer is simple, **take issue** with the ideas, concepts, approaches and techniques of Dr. Richard O'Connell. I will not be offended, hurt, and embarrassed at my ineptness, my way out point of view, my naiveté, etc... I will not be there! I will not even know I am being criticized or praised. The beauty of it all is no one will feel that any of the "slings and arrows" are directed toward them, since my advice is not directed at any one individual person in the group.

However, the abuse or agreement heaped on the author must be done in the following manner: the dialogue must take place **horizontally, not vertically.** That is to say, each group in the school community must look to see how <u>they as a group</u> can contribute to guidance services rather than making recommendations on how counselors must change. Select a chapter or concept from the handbook that pertains to your group and toss it out for evaluation. There is plenty of material with which to disagree or agree. In the handbook, there is a chapter specifically for each member group of the school community to analyze or discuss.

The purpose of the dialogue is for each group to concentrate on internal changes and not to concentrate on the flaws of other groups in the school community. If you take the **vertical approach,** you are back to square one, requesting changes for other people in a system that is already set in its ways. The suggestions made from any group outside the guidance department for the guidance department, will have counselors saying, "What does the PTA, Board of Ed., teachers, administrators, department heads, etc. know about the intricacies and demands of guidance?" Vertical dialogue is inquisitional, an effort to find out what is wrong with the guidance department and then try to correct it. Rather, the group should be looking honestly at itself to make productive changes, which contribute to guidance services and ultimately benefit the student body. With the horizontal approach, collectively there will be more changes across the board for the good of the guidance department and students. This is not to say that the horizontal approach will solve every problem or radically change personnel in the guidance department, but it will move the guidance department forward.

The more effective horizontal approach presupposes a collaborative agreement among the members of the school to work together by enhancing services to students through Guidance Services. It is very healthy when each group decides on an internal change that they can communicate to the rest of the school community. This openness expresses to the school community that the group is willing to change and invites the rest of the community to do likewise. Naturally, it should be the **Guidance Department** that should make the first statement. It would be an obvious sign to the rest of the school that internal changes in guidance are being made to improve services to students. The natural opening for this announcement could be, "Based on our analysis of the book <u>Improving School Guidance Services</u>, we the members of the guidance department so as **to improve services to students** have set as one of our goals to be more visible in the hallways, etc." Or, "The guidance department will seek more collaborative teamwork with teachers regarding the placement of students, etc."

Ideally, the other member groups of the school community (PTA, administration, secretaries, SEPTA, Board of Ed., the various departments, etc.) would make a similar declaration regarding their internal changes. Note the emphasis on **improving services to students** rather than targeting individual counselors to change. These statements may be published in the principal's weekly bulletin, superintendent's newsletter, or, more privately, a written communiqué to the Director of Guidance to be shared with the counselors:

"People who work together will win, whether it is against complex football defenses or the problems of modern society." Vince Lombardi (Chosen by Peter O'Connell)

The following chapters are suggested for horizontal dialogue **within** each group:

1. Administrators to administrators, Chapter 4, 10

2. Teachers to teachers in various departments, Chapter 5, etc.

3. Parent groups to one another, Chapter 3, etc.

4. As a discussion group for SEPTA members, Chapter 6, etc.

5. As a topic for School Superintendent's Day for all departments using the horizontal method.

6. As part of a department meetings, Chapter 5

7. As a topic for the PTA members, Chapter 3, and chapters that refer to present concerns

8. As a topic for the of Board of Ed., Chapter 10, 4

9. Graduate interns and their college professor. Chapters 1-29

10. As an one on one discussion, counselor to guidance department head, Chapters 1-29

11. Counselors to counselors, Chapter 1-29

In selecting a chapter, technique, approach, or concept from the book, do not be devious. Do not make it "a set up" aimed at a particular counselor. It becomes obvious to a group member when a topic is directly pointing to that person; even the best of ideas are blocked in this environment. Defenses go up; an internal, oppositional posture is subconsciously taken. Rather, select the whole chapter in which the topic is included so that it becomes part of the normal discussion. The more objective the discussion, the more chances there are for change.

A Collegial Horizontal Method for Improving School Guidance Services

A suggested way to get the whole school community on board to help improve guidance services is to introduce it as a collegial endeavor. The Collegial Method uses the horizontal approach wherein each group in the school community makes internal improvements, which contribute to guidance services. Once it is understood that the improvements come from within each group through the analysis of Dr. O'Connell's handbook and the chapters that apply to each group, there will be less apprehension on the part of the school community.

How It Can Be Done

Whoever is sponsoring the dialogue (an administrator, guidance chairperson or pupil personnel director) it is suggested to buy a small quantity of <u>Improving School Guidance Services.</u> (This is not a sales pitch.) Each group is then asked to read a specific chapter or the whole book to get an overview. The group then comes together to discuss their chapter, and then makes a statement of their discussions, similar to the examples given above. A simple statement from the PTA or SEPTA that, "They have obtained a greater understanding and appreciation of guidance secretaries, and understand that at times secretaries are overloaded," will have a positive effect. Similarly, the PTA (SEPTA) may comment that they see a need to build a core of volunteers to help in the guidance office when called upon. Or, as suggested earlier the PTA can advocate for a free SAT course to be offered for its student body. Administrators may decide to invite a counselor representative to be on their pre-planning team for academic development. Again, administrators may indicate that they realize there is a great deal of good, hidden work the counselors effect in students lives which contribute to academic growth. Again, they indicate that fewer problems come their way when counselors have sufficient time to examine schedules and to place students so that there are less teacher conflicts. The ELL coordinator may voice that students are happiest when placed in an environment by their counselor which is accepting and nurturing.

Should a group feel it should have a vertical dialogue with the guidance department regarding certain chapters in the book; a request should be made to the guidance department chairperson to determine its feasibility. This should take place after the group's positive statement. If the atmosphere is conducive and the chairperson agrees, the discussion should be collegial, objective, and positive and referenced to the handbook, Improving School Guidance Services.

Again, discuss chapters not the faults of the department. The collegial approach will help improve many aspects of guidance services....not all. However, this approach goes beyond the concept that all guidance services emanate from the guidance office. After all, is it not the job of all school staff to support and "guide" the development of each and every student? The collegial approach will bring about changes that are internalized and enduring across the school community.

*****

The title of this epilogue is **How to Use This Book.** May I suggest another use? There are certain chapters which when revised according to the practices of your guidance department, could be used as a monthly bulletin to inform new staff and refresh experienced members on various guidance procedures and practices. It is a false conception that all the complex procedures within the guidance department are known and understood by all the staff. A well-done monthly bulletin will serve as a great public relations vehicle and educational tool. If a specific chapter of value to the guidance department is chosen and the department shapes it into a bulletin, the task would be easy to accomplish. Chapters that refer to other departments (Special Education, English Language Learners, etc.) may be shaped into a bulletin jointly by the guidance department and each of the other departments. At the end of the school year, these bulletins may be collated into a guidance manual for the following year.

******

*In the copyright section of the handbook it states, "No part of this book may be duplicated." That's what it says and that's what is meant. However, there are exceptions for the following reasons:

1. For those districts that cannot afford it, you may obtain permission to duplicate chapters. It is more important that change be brought about for the good of students. The author has deliberately kept the price of the book low in terms of today's market to minimize the cost to graduate students and schools.

2. The integrity of the decision is up to the district. If the chapters are to be duplicated, simply have an administrator contact www. dr.roconnell33@yahoo.com for permission to duplicate, which will be automatically given. The author is more interested in knowing who is using the book than requiring permission.

3. For those guidance departments that wish to produce a monthly bulletin based on various chapters in the book, be the author's guest. The one request is that the title of the book with its web site www. schoolguidancesrvices.com are noted in the bulletin and an e-mail copy is sent to dr.roconnell33@yahoo.com The author would like to learn more about the practices of other guidance departments and possibly use some of the ideas in a revised edition of this handbook.

4. For those districts that can afford it, the copyright for producing chapters applies. Another advantage in purchasing a small quantity of handbooks (Again, this is not a sales pitch.) is that each member of the

school community will read the whole book and get a total overview of the counselors' work. Additionally, it is a lot cheaper than hiring a guidance consultant and the chances of real internal change with the book are greater and more comprehensive. A more diverse number of school community members can be reached. The books may be purchased in bulk at a discounted rate through the web site: www. schoolguidanceservices.com

ADDENDUM 1

An Actual Sample of the Diversified Duties of A Counselor over a Five-Day Period

COUNSELOR LOG

"A Week in the Life of a Guidance Counselor"

The following log encompasses all the varied activities and responsibilities in a typical week of a Guidance Counselor (3/19—3/23). It was prepared to share the diverse nature of a counselor's work:

College searches on the internet.

Verification for a Federal Government Parental Background check.

Tutorials set up for students.

Parental notification for special SAT accommodations for children with learning disabilities.

Calls to colleges to advocate for students.

Counseling a student rejected by a college.

Counseling a suicidal student.

Setting up program schedules.

Admitting a new ESL student.

Follow up on the adjustment of an ESL student.

Planning next year's schedule with 9, 10, and 11 graders.

Parent contact to set up a "G.E.D. Springboard" program.

Placement of a student at the E.A.C. program.

Recommendation to a parent for a student in need of a psychiatric referral.

Assist in the programming of 8th grade students.

Preparing special forms for the Annual Review of Special Education Students.

Attending C.S. E. meetings.

Attending P.P.S. meeting with follow up responsibilities.

Supplying New York Court ordered materials.

Conferring with Special Education Director regarding students.

Junior College Parent Interviews—planning sessions.

Beginning work on college recommendations for next year's seniors.

Advising seniors on the FAFSA and the Profile.

Processing BOCES applications and withdrawals.

Monitor BOCES attendance.

Processing "Progress Reports".

Emergency suicide ideation threat and referral.

Referral to PPS of a student who is hostile and destructively vengeful

Assisting in "Decisions for Life Program".

Conferring with BOCES principal on a troubled student.

Scholarship application process.

Conferring with the Guidance Director on graduation requirements for a doubtful Student

Updating BOCES roster.

Obtaining correct names from seniors for their graduation diploma

Conferring with G.E.D. program director regarding a student

Working with a Spanish translator for a student whose parent only speaks Spanish.

Follow up on an "at risk" student.

Request for a level change on an academic schedule

Parental phone call on a student not doing homework and failing to report to the

Homework Center

Request from a parent to expedite a scholarship application

Request from a dropped out student to make up lost credits to graduate

A call to a neighboring high school to do a background check on a transferring student

Meeting with E.L.L. teacher to hand schedule E.L.L. students.

Meeting with the principal to recognize "at risk" students who are doing well.

Planning for an E.L.L. brunch to assist E.L.L. students in their adjustment to their new school

Planning with a parent for the transition of an L.D. student to college.

Check out waiver of time limits on SAT exam.

Conferring with a therapist regarding a student.

Conferred with school psychologist on a student with parental problems.

Conferred with math department head on a teacher-student conflict.

Providing a tutor for a student.

Call an irate parent regarding her son being picked on.

Dealing with a minority student and Urban League Scholarship.

Early morning hall presence to greet faculty and students.

Preparing for preliminary C.S.E. meetings.

Advise staff member on possible parent-teacher confrontation.

Work through a teacher-student conflict.

Contact attendance office on an out of district placement

Check out Detention Room to confer with students.

Write a letter for a student seeking employment.

Review graduation qualifications for seniors.

Advising staff on college matters.

Prepare a letter to parents of L.D. students regarding a college visit to C.W. Post's Support Program.

Working with secretaries on various projects, which relate to the above.

ADDENDUM 2

"The Counselor's External Office"
Published in the NY Nassau County Counselors' Journal, "THE NEWSCASTER" By Dr. Richard O'Connell

As a counselor: Do you wish to increase your contact with students?

Do you wish to increase your faculty contacts?

Do you wish to increase your efficiency and decrease your workload?

Do you wish to increase your knowledge of students based on their physical appearance?

Do you wish to increase the guidance public relations effort in your school?

Do you wish to have your students realize you really care about them?

Do you wish to deliver efficiently more service to your students?

Then stand in a central place: entrance to school, outside your office or in a main corridor each day, a half-hour before school begins and greets both students and staff. This practice takes a little courage and self-discipline to get to your self-appointed post each day. Over the years, I have come to value this procedure, so I take the time in a very busy day to achieve this goal. The courage part comes when you assume a piece of hallway turf and staff question why you are there. It takes courage to reach out and begin to greet your students and fellow faculty members with a "good morning." The advantage of this procedure is that eventually both faculty and students know you are there, especially new teachers: to help answer questions, to give advice, to share small talk or just to say hello.

From the point of view of the student, the procedure affords the counselor the opportunity to assess student affect. This is a valuable opportunity since students can change in appearance from day to day and indicate to us if they are troubled or demonstrating a change of behavior. A few examples from my experience will suffice. When a student changes from a usually upbeat youngster into a withdrawn or sad individual, you have an external warning. When you see students arriving late, there is a problem. When you see a couple coming to school each day forming a new relationship, it is valuable information; or equally significant is a sudden disappearance of one member of the couple. There have been cases when students were depressed and suicidal and it was assessed in the hallway. When students break a bone, you have immediate knowledge. All the visual clues you pick up as first hand information feeds back to your dealings with parents and students during the normal course of the day.

Likewise, it is amazing how much of your work can be done in the hallway. By nature of our profession, we are constantly requesting students to follow up:

Are forms returned?

Are students reminded to live up to expectations?

Are students reminded that assignments are due?

Are students praised?

A sentence or two can accomplish each of theses tasks. It is difficult to interview all of your students, especially if your caseload is in the hundreds, who are doing poorly as revealed in a review of their report cards or progress reports. Standing in the hallway affords the opportunity of seeing many and giving them encouragement or advice. For most students, a friendly hello will suffice. For those who need a reminder just your presence may trigger a response. By the way, a friendly hello in the morning may be the postscript to a horrific family experience the night before. Above all, your presence in the hallway, greeting students with a kind hello is a statement to the students that you care about them. I am sure this message is conveyed in other ways during the day as well, but the opportunity to reach more kids is increased by your presence in the hallway.

Regarding the faculty, they are on the run for the most part. Your presence in their path along the way to their classrooms gives them easy access to discuss a student, ask for a conference, or fill you in on a particular problem. These exchanges are made more difficult if a formal meeting has to be scheduled. It is also more time consuming. Even substitute teachers appreciate someone to turn to in negotiating the intricacies of a new school. This accessibility has had tangential side effects. It establishes a good rapport with staff. For counselors to function effectively in any school, we need the cooperation and support of our staff to assist our students.

From the point of view of the administration, they appreciate the backup in the hallway. I have never been asked to function as a monitor. Rather, administrators appreciate the "reach out" effort of a counselor who is not closeted in his/her covey hole, "secreted away" from the main flow. The public relations aspect of the "external office" is obvious.

In conclusion, the "Counselor's External Office" brings more service to students. It makes the counselor more accessible. It establishes a rapport with staff and conveys a very caring concern to students. It establishes an atmosphere of involvement and helps to break down barriers. It maximizes the use of our time, so much so I stand at my "post" whenever I can shake free during my busy day. In addition to all these attributes, it has become for me...... great deal of fun.

ADDENDUM 3

A Directory of Whom to Contact

School Directories

Guidance counselors are often times called upon to supply information that is not in their domain. If counselors allow themselves to become the messenger service for the rest of the school, then they will be called upon incessantly to supply information. Not only that, but the counselors have allowed themselves to become **responsible** for this information. An arrangement should be worked out with administration to clarify the role of each area of school responsibility. Once this is done, "**A Directory of Whom to Contact**" should be published. It is then easy for the counselor to refer a call for information to the right office. All schools have a directory. **A Directory of Whom to Contact** lists phone numbers by the services required and is more specific than the school directory.

Area of Information	Office to Call	Tel.No.
For transcripts and previous letters of recommendation	Guidance Secretary	_____
Advice on course information	Guidance Counselor(s)	_____
Advice on schedule changes	Guidance Counselor(s)	_____
BOCES information	Guidance Counselor(s)	_____
Request for a Parent/Teacher Meeting	Main Office	____etc.____
Request for a Counselor Meeting	Guidance Counselor(s)	
Counselor/Teacher Meeting	Guidance Counselor(s)	
Request for Progress Reports	Guidance Secretary	
Request for School Psychologist	School Psychologist	
Special Education Teacher	Special Education Secretary	
Request for an IEP and psychological report	School Psychologist	
Request for special education information	Dept. of Special Education	
Request for reports card	Guidance Secretaries	
Messages to students from parent	Main Office	
Request to deliver a book or lunch money, etc.	Main Office	
Request for cutting and absentee information	Attendance Office	
Request for yearbook pictures	Yearbook Moderator	
Request for cap & gown information	Graduation Coordinator	
Request for Bus Information	Bus Office	
Health related matters	Nurse's Office	
Physical Education information	P.E. Office	
Student's PE teacher	Boys' Gym Girls' Gym Office	

ADDENDUM 4

Sample College Profiles

The World of Academic Reality

The following sample college profiles are examples of the general requirements for college admissions at real colleges with fictitious names. They are offered here for parents to review and for students to do a self-assessment and to ascertain their chances of getting into a specific college. This type of profile as well as other college profiles can lead parents and students to the world of academic reality. Profiles are updated each year and can generally be viewed on the college web site. In reading college profiles, other factors must be kept in mind. The numbers listed are the general parameters of acceptance and do not include other factors (extraordinary achievements, special circumstances, etc.) which will be factored into the acceptance equation.

Sample 1

COLLEGE NAME: *The College of Fun & Games*	Admission statistics			Credentials of admitted students		
	Year			Year		
	I	II	III	I	II	III
Applications	6268	6059	6050			
Accepts	2108	2238	2275			
Enrolled	756	778	715			
EARLY DECISION						
APPLICATIONS	613	486	459			
ACCEPTS	300	289	237			
ENROLLED	290	281	231			
mid 50% SAT v				640-720	640-720	630-710
mid 50% SAT				650-730	650-720	640-720
mid 50% ACT				28-32	29-32	27-31
AVERAGE GPA				3.65	3.61	3.60
TOP 20%				93%	91%	91.5%
Students of color	143	122	98			
International enrolled	48	40	30			
Legacy enrolled	57	60	51			

Sample 2

COLLEGE NAME: *The College of Hard Knocks*

VOLUME OF APPLICATIONS

Early Decision Applications	1,918
Regular Decision Applications	12.688
Total Applications	14,606
Early Decision Acceptances	506
Early Decision Acceptance Rate	26%)
April Acceptances	1,928
Total Acceptances	2,434
Overall Admit Rate	16.7%
Anticipated Class Size	1,430

Date by which April Accepts must reply:

CLASS RANK INFORMATION

		APPLIED	Acc%	Ace
Valedictorian	1,112			369
Salutatorian	33%			
Other top 5%		540	148	27%
Total top 10%		3,466	602	17%
		6,329	1,259	20%

97% of accepted students are in the top 10% of their graduating classes; 43% of the accepted class attend high schools that do not rank students; over 6,000 students applied from schools that do not rank students.

SAT I PERCENTILE DATA
Middle 50th Percentile scores for accepted students:
Verbal: 650-760   Math: 670 - 770

TYPE OF SCHOOL ATTENDED	NUMBER	% of ACCEPTED CLASS
	Public	
Private		812 (33%)
Parochial/Religious		199 (8%)

91 students attend schools not coded with type of school.

GENDER	ACCEPTED CLASS
Men	1,069 (44%)
Women	1,365 (56%)

ETHNICITY	
African Amen can	226 (9%)
Asian American	379 (16%)
Latino	196 (8%)
Native American	15 (<1%)
White	1,047 (43%)
Unknown	387 (16%)
Foreign Citizens	184 (8%)

GEOGRAPHIC AREA	
Northern New England	80 (3%)
Southern New England	436 (18%)
Middle Atlantic	329 (14%.)
New York	333 (14%)
Mid West	183 (8%)
Central	32 (1%)
Mountain	77 (3%)
California	320 (13%)
Pacific	73 (3%)
Southern	315 (13%)
Territories	11 (<1%)
International	245 (10%)

GEOGRAPHICAL DISTRIBUTION	
From Rhode Island	99 (4%)
From New England	417 (17%)
Outside New England	1,673 (69%)
Foreign Countries	245 (10%)
States represented	49
Countries represented	55

ACADEMIC INTERESTS	
Engineering	256 (11%)
The Humanities	603 (25%)
Math and Science	904 (37%)
Social Sciences	439 (18%))
Undecided	232 (10%)

DEGREE CHOICE	
Bachelor of Ails	1,568 (64%)
Bachelor of Science	678 (28%)
PLME	103 (4%)
Accept Out of PLME	85 (4%)

1. Children of Alumni 162 (7 %)

ADDENDUM 5

SUBMITTING THE COLLEGE APPLICATION

Students, who have completed their college application, are to fill out this form for each college and attach it to each application submitted.

Be sure to attach the following to the college application cover page:

1. Teacher recommendation(s) _____ 2. Essay (if applicable)_

3. Activity sheet_____ 4. Resume_____

COLLEGE APPLICATION COVER PAGE

Name of Student_____

Soc.Sec. #_____

Name of College/Scholarship_____

_____

Address of College/Program_____ _____

_____

What kind of application: Early Decision, Early Action, Rolling / Regular

Admissions _____

Deadline date_____

Is your application fee (check) attached? (Circle) Yes No

Have you paid by credit card? Yes No

Have you requested your SAT I/II or ACT scores to be sent to colleges?

Yes No

Date the tests were last taken: _____

_____

Have you checked this application and is it complete? Yes No

Do you waive your right to read the counselor's recommendation? Yes

No

Student's Signature_____

_____

Parent's Signature_____

Date received by the counselor_____

Counselor's Signature_____

Date of Mailing (Office Use Only) _____

Copies: To the student's college file_____
To the student for personal record _____

SAMPLE POST CARDS TO BE INCLUDED
IN EACH APPLICATION

The benefit of including two post cards (one addressed to the guidance office and the other self-addressed to the student) is that missing information is immediately identified. When post cards are received indicating that all material has been sent, future complications are prevented. Often when information is missing, there is a lengthy time delay before the college notifies the applicant. The enclosed post cards speeds up the process. At other times, some colleges do not notify students and it is only after the applicant inquires that the cause for the delay is found. When information is missing, the guidance counselor is generally blamed. With the post card system, whatever is missing is quickly identified and sent, speeding up the student's review and obviating serious complaints.

POST CARD ADDRESSED TO THE GUIDANCE OFFICE

****

Date_____

Records for (Name) _____

1. The application packet is complete and has been received in our Admissions Office_____

2. The following items are missing: a._____

_____

b._____

_____

Name of College_____

_____

****

POST CARD ADDRESSED TO THE STUDENT'S HOME

****

Date_____

_____

Records for (Name)_____

_____

1. The application packet is complete and has been received in our
Admissions Office _____

_____

2. The following items are missing: a._____

_____

b._____

_____

Name of College_____

_____

****

ADDENDUM 6

The College Interview Sheet

This suggested interview sheet is only as good as the counselor's skills at drawing out information from the student. The counselor should probe each topic to reveal possible achievements that do not immediately come to the mind of the student. It is meant as an "interview sheet" and not as a questionnaire to be filled out by the student. The information collected should become the basis for a good college recommendation as well as provide information for the counselor to act upon.

The "College Interview Sheet" should be explained individually to each student at a personal interview session. The counselor fills it out, not the student. Have the student relax and feel comfortable to mention anything that comes to mind, no matter how insignificant. From little bits of information, the counselor may garner a theme or a different approach to presenting the student in the recommendation.

THE COLLEGE INTERVIEW SHEET

This Sheet Will Be Used in Writing Your College Recommendation

Student's Name_____GPA____

_____

Special Personal Qualities_____

_____

Jobs Held_____

_____

Special Circumstances_____

_____

Special Talents_____

_____

Leadership_____

_____

Special Awards: Athletic, Social, Academic_____

_____

Out of School Activities_____

_____

Special Courses_____

_____

Volunteer Work_____

_____

Teams and Clubs_____

_____

Special Hobbies_____

_____

What colleges are you considering?

1._____2_____3._____4._____

5._____6._____7._____8._____

What teachers you will ask for college recommendations:

1._____2._____

3._____4._____

Do you waive your right to read the recommendation? (Circle) Yes No

Student's signature_____

ADDENDUM 7

IBO INTERNATIONAL BACCALAUREATE ORGANIZATION

The Diploma Programme of the International Baccalaureate Organization (IBO) is a demanding pre-university course of study that leads to examinations; it is designed for highly motivated secondary school students aged 16 to 19. The programme incorporates the best elements of national systems without being based on any one. The ISO's goal is to provide students with the values and opportunities that will enable them to develop sound judgment, make wise decisions and respect others in the global community. In the 30 years since its founding, the IB diploma has become a symbol of academic integrity and intellectual promise. The student who satisfies its demands demonstrates a strong commitment to learning, both in terms of the mastery of subject content and in the development of the skills and discipline necessary for success in a competitive world. Colleges and universities do well to encourage the enrollment of these able young scholars.

The Curriculum
The Diploma Programme curriculum consists of six subject groups.

Group 1: language A1
Language A1
First language including the study of selections from world literature.

Group 2: second language
Language A2
A language and literature course for fluent or bilingual students

Language B

Language *ab initio* classical languages

A foreign language course for students with previous experience of the language.

A foreign language courses for beginners: Classical Greek, Latin

Group 3 individual and societies

History, geography economics, philosophy, social and cultural anthropology, business and management, information technology in a global society, Islamic history

Group 4 experimental sciences

Biology, chemistry, physics environmental systems SL, design technology

Group 5: mathematics and computer science

Mathematics H L, math methods SL, math studies SL, further mathematics SL,

computer science (elective only)

Group 6: Visual arts, theatre, music

Diploma and Certificate

Diploma Programme candidates are required to study six subjects: one subject from each of groups 1 to 5 and a sixth subject from group 6 or an elective. The electives include a second subject from groups 1 to 4, further mathematics SL, computer science and a school-based syllabus approved by the IBO. At least three and not more than four of the six subjects are taken at higher level (HL), the others at standard level (SL). Each subject is graded on a scale of 1 (minimum) to 7 (maximum). The award of the diploma requires candidates to meet defined standards and conditions. These include a minimum total of 24 points and the satisfactory completion of three additional requirements: the extended essay of some 4,000 words, which provides a first experience of preparing an independent research paper; a course entitled theory of knowledge (TOK), which is an interdisciplinary requirement intended to stimulate critical reflection on knowledge and experience gained inside and outside the classroom; and the compulsory participation in CAS—creativity, action, service.

Approximately 80% of candidates are awarded the diploma. A candidate who does not satisfy the requirements of the full Diploma Programme, or who has elected to take fewer than six subjects, is awarded a certificate for the examinations completed. Diploma candidates who complete more than six subjects receive an extra certificate for the additional subject(s).

Grading and Results

A candidate's examination performance in individual subjects is graded according to the following scale.

7. Excellent
6. Very good
5. Good
4. Satisfactory
3. Mediocre
2. Poor
1. Very poor
N. NO Grade

The TOK course and the extended essay are graded according to this scale.

A. Excellent
B. Good
C. Satisfactory
D. Mediocre
E. Elementary
N. No grade

The Diploma Programme candidate's six subjects can yield 42 points. Three further points are available for the combination of the extended essay and work in TOK. Therefore, the maximum possible score is 45 points. Results are available in mid-July for May examination session candidates, and mid-January for November examination session candidates. If requested, an official transcript of results will be sent to universities. The transcript will indicate the level of the subjects, the grade awarded in each, the total points scored and the completion of the additional diploma requirements. It is typically marked **diploma awarded or certificate awarded.** The **bilingual diploma awarded** indicates that the candidate has studied two languages A1, or has studied a language A1 and a language A2, or has taken an examination in at least one subject from group 3 or group 4 in a language other than his or her language A1.

Authorization and Recognition

Only schools officially authorized by the IBO may offer the Diploma Programme and present candidates for examination. There are over 1,400 participating schools in more than 110 countries. Of these, about one-third are located in the United States, Canada or the Caribbean, and one-third in the Africa/Europe/Middle East region.

The IBO has shown that students are well prepared for university work and the Diploma Programme has earned a reputation for rigorous assessment, giving IB diploma holders access to the world's leading universities. These include institutions such as Cambridge, Harvard, Heidelberg, McGill, MIT, Oxford, Princeton, Rotterdam Erasmus, Sorbonne, UBC and Yale.

The IBO is based in Geneva, Switzerland, with regional offices in Geneva, New York, Buenos Aires and Singapore. The curriculum and assessment centre, located in Cardiff, Wales, United Kingdom, oversees two examination sessions per year. The May session serves the majority of candidates, who are from schools in the northern hemisphere; the November session caters for schools in the southern hemisphere. Over 5,000 examiners worldwide, under the supervision of chief examiners renowned in their fields, are involved in the assessment of candidate work.

Universities requiring additional information are invited to contact the nearest regional office:

NORTH AMERICA & CARIBBEAN Code: **IBNA** Mr Bradley W Richardson, regional director IBO North America, USA Tel: 1212 696 4464 Fax :1212 889 9242 e-mail: ibna@ibo.org

ADDENDUM 8

Steps in Applying for Aid
Using the Online FAFSA

GET A PIN

Before beginning the FAFSA, you should apply for *a* U.S. Department of Education personal identification number (PIN) at www.pin.ed.gov. The PIN will allow you to sign your FAFSA electronically and to correct your processed FAFSA information online. After you receive the PIN assigned to you, we recommend you change it to something easy to remember. Don't share your PIN with anyone! If you are providing parent information on the FAFSA, one of your parents must also sign your application. To sign electronically, your parent must apply for his or her own PIN.

GATHER THE INFORMATION REQUIRED TO APPLY

Your Social Security number and your parents' Social Security numbers if you are providing parent information

Your driver's license number if you have one

Your Alien Registration Number if you are not a U.S. citizen

Federal tax information or tax returns, including W-2 information, for yourself, for your spouse if you are married, and for your parents if you are providing parent information, using income records for the year prior to the academic year for which you are applying

Records of untaxed income, such as Social Security benefits. Temporary Assistance for Needy Families (TANF), and veterans benefits, for yourself (and for your parents if you are providing parent information); and information on savings, investments, and business and farm assets for yourself (and for your parents if you are providing parent information)BE AWARE OF DEADLINES

You may have to meet application deadlines, depending on your college and where you live. State and school deadlines are usually earlier than federal deadlines.

USE THE FAFSA ON THE WEB WORKSHEET
Your college or high school might have a copy of the *Worksheet, or* you can print one from www.fafsa.ed.gov. This *Worksheet* is optional, but it will help you collect the information you need to fill out your FAFSA online.

COMPLETE YOUR APPLICATION AT WWW.FAFSA. ED.GOV
Enter all necessary information. If you need help, there are help links on each page of the online application.

SUBMIT YOUR APPLICATION
After you submit your application, make sure you receive a confirmation number. This number tells you your application has been successfully submitted. Keep this confirmation number for your records.

FOLLOW UP ON YOUR FAFSA
Your application will be processed and you will receive an e-mail with a link to your *Student Aid Report* (SAR). If you did not provide an e-mail address, you will receive your SAR by mail. You should review your SAR for any necessary corrections or updates. If you do not hear from us within three weeks, go to www.fafsa.ed.gov and select: "Check the Status of a Submitted FAFSA."

ADDENDUM 9

Students with Disabilities Preparing for Post Secondary Education:
Know Your Rights and Responsibilities

Reproduction and ordering information:
U.S. Department of Education
Margaret Spellings Secretary
Office for Civil Rights
James Manning *Delegated the Authority of Assistant Secretary*
First published July 2002. Reprinted May 2004. Revised May 2005.

U.S. Department of Education Office for Civil Rights Washington, D.C. 2020 More and more high school students with disabilities are planning to continue their education in postsecondary schools, including vocational and career schools, two- and four-year colleges, and universities. As a student with a disability, you need to be well informed about your rights and responsibilities as well as the responsibilities that postsecondary schools have toward you. Being well informed will help ensure that you have a full opportunity to enjoy the benefits of the postsecondary education experience without confusion or delay.

The Office for Civil Rights (OCR) in the U.S. Department of Education is providing the information in this pamphlet to explain the rights and responsibilities of students with disabilities who are preparing to attend postsecondary schools. This pamphlet also explains the obligations of a postsecondary school to provide academic adjustments, including auxiliary aids and services, to ensure that the school does not discriminate on the basis of disability. OCR enforces Section 504 of the Rehabilitation Act of 1973 (Section 504) and Title II of the Americans with Disabilities Act of 1990 (Title II), which prohibit discrimination on the basis of disability. Practically every school district and postsecondary school in the United States is subject to one or both of these laws, which have similar requirements.*Because both school districts and postsecondary schools must comply with these same laws, you and your parents might believe that postsecondary schools and school districts have the same responsibilities. This is not true; the responsibilities of postsecondary schools are significantly different from those of school districts. Moreover, you will have responsibilities as a postsecondary student that you do not have as a high school student. OCR strongly encourages you to know your responsibilities and those of postsecondary schools under Section 504 and Title II. Doing so will improve your opportunity to succeed as you enter postsecondary education. The following questions and answers provide more specific information to help you succeed.

As a student with a disability leaving high school and entering postsecondary education, will I see differences in my rights and how they are addressed?

Yes. Section 504 and Title II protect elementary, secondary and postsecondary students from discrimination. Nevertheless, several of the requirements that apply through high school are different from the requirements that apply beyond high school. For instance, Section 504 requires a school district to provide a free appropriate public education (FAPE) to each child with a disability in the district's jurisdiction. Whatever the disability, a school district must identify an individual's education needs and provide any regular or special education and related aids and services necessary to meet those needs as well as it is meeting the needs of students without disabilities.

Schools may set reasonable standards for documentation. Some schools require more documentation than others. They may require you to provide documentation prepared by an appropriate professional, such as a medical doctor, psychologist or other qualified diagnostician. The required documentation may include one or more of the following: a diagnosis of your current disability; the date of the diagnosis; how the diagnosis was reached; the credentials of the professional; how your disability affects a major life activity; and how the disability affects your academic performance. The documentation should provide enough information for you and your school to decide what is an appropriate academic adjustment.

Although an Individualized Education Program (IEP) or Section 504 plan, if you have one, may help identify services that have been effective for you, it generally is not sufficient documentation. This is because postsecondary education presents different demands than high school education, and what you need to meet these new demands may be different. Also in some cases, the nature of a disability may change.

If the documentation that you have does not meet the postsecondary school's requirements, a school official must tell you in a timely manner what additional documentation you need to provide. You may need a new evaluation in order to provide the required documentation.

Who has to pay for a new evaluation?

Neither your high school nor your postsecondary school is required to conduct or pay for a new evaluation to document your disability and need for an academic adjustment. This may mean that you have to pay or find funding to pay an appropriate professional to do it. If you are eligible for services through your state vocational rehabilitation agency, you may qualify for an evaluation at no cost to you. You may locate your state vocational rehabilitation agency through this Department of Education Web page: http://www.ed.gpv/about/off1ces/list/osers/rsa/index.html

Once the school has received the necessary documentation from me, what should I expect?

The school will review your request in light of the essential requirements for the relevant program to help determine an appropriate academic adjustment. It is important to remember that the school is not required to lower or waive essential requirements. If you have requested a specific academic adjustment, the school may offer that academic adjustment or an alternative one if the alternative also would be effective. The school may also conduct its own evaluation of your disability and needs at its own expense.

You should expect your school to work with you in an interactive process to identify an appropriate academic adjustment. Unlike the experience you may have had in high school, however, do not expect your postsecondary school to invite your parents to participate in the process or to develop an IEP for you.

What if the academic adjustment we identified is not working?

Let the school know as soon as you become aware that the results are not what you expected. It may be too late to correct the problem if you wait until the course or activity is completed. You and your school should work together to resolve the problem.

May a postsecondary school charge me for providing an academic adjustment?

No. Furthermore, it may not charge students with disabilities more for participating in its programs or activities than it charges students who do not have disabilities.

What can I do if I believe the school is discriminating against me?

Practically every postsecondary school must have a person— frequently called the Section 504 Coordinator, ADA Coordinator, or Disability Services Coordinator—who coordinates the school's compliance with Section 504 or Title II or both laws. You may contact this person for information about how to address your concerns.

The school also must have grievance procedures. These procedures are not the same as the due process procedures with which you may be familiar from high school. However, the postsecondary school's grievance procedures must include steps to ensure that you may raise your concerns fully and fairly and must provide for the prompt and equitable resolution of complaints.

School publications, such as student handbooks and catalogs, usually describe the steps you must take to start the grievance process. Often, schools have both formal and informal processes. If you decide to use a grievance process, you should be prepared to present all the reasons that support your request.

If you are dissatisfied with the outcome from using the school's grievance procedures or you   wish to pursue an alternative to using the grievance procedures, you may file a complaint against the school with OCR or in a court. You may learn more about the OCR complaint process from the brochure *How to File a Discrimination Complaint with the Office for Civil Rights,* which you may obtain by contacting us at the addresses and phone numbers below, or at http://www.ed.gov/ocr/dQCS/hpwtQ.html.

If you would like more information about the responsibilities of postsecondary schools to students with disabilities, read the OCR brochure *Auxiliary Aids and Services for Postsecondary Students with Disabilities: Higher Education's Obligations Under Section 504 and Title II of the ADA.* You may obtain a copy by contacting us at the address and phone numbers below, or at http://www.ed.gov/ocr/docs/auxaids.htmj.

Students with disabilities who know their rights and responsibilities are much better equipped to succeed in postsecondary school. We encourage you to work with the staff at your school because they, too, want you to succeed. Seek the support of family, friends and fellow students, including those with disabilities. Know your talents and capitalize on them, and believe in yourself as you embrace new challenges in your education.

To receive more information about the civil rights of students with disabilities in education institutions, contact us at:

Customer Service Team
Office for Civil Rights
U.S. Department of Education
Washington, D.C. 20202-1100
Phone: 1-800-421-3481
TDD: 1- 877-521-2172
Email: pcr@ed.goy
Web site: www.ed.gov/ocr

You may be familiar with another federal law that applies to the education of students with disabilities—the Individuals with Disabilities Education Act (IDEA). That law is administered by the Office of Special Education Programs in the Office of Special Education and Rehabilitative Services in the U.S. Department of Education. The IDEA and its Individualized Education Program (IEP) provisions do not apply to postsecondary schools. This pamphlet does not discuss the IDEA or state and local laws that may apply.

This publication is in the public domain. Authorization to reproduce it in whole or in part is granted. The publication's citation should be: U.S. Department of Education, Office for Civil Rights, *Students with Disabilities Preparing for Postsecondary Education: Know Your Rights and Responsibilities,* Washington, D.C., 2005.
To order copies of this publication, write:
ED Pubs
Education Publications Center
U.S. Department of Education

RICHARD O'CONNELL, ED. D.

P.O. Box 1398

Jessup, MD 20794-1398

You may fax your order to: 301-470-1244 or send an e-mail request to: edpubs@inet.ed.gov

You may also call toll-free: 1-877-433-7827 (1-877-4-ED-PUBS). If 877 service is not yet available in your area, call 1-800-872-5327 (1-800-USA-LEARN). Those who use a telecommunications device for the deaf (TDD) or a teletypewriter (TTY), should call 1-877-576-7734.

To order online, point your Internet browser to: www.edpubs.org

This publication is also available on the Department's Web site at http://www.ed.gov/ocr/transition.html.

Any updates to this publication will be available at this Web site. On request, this publication is also available in alternate formats, such as Braille, large print, or computer diskette. For more information, please contact the Department's Alternate Format Center 202-260-9895 or (202) 260-0818.

ADDENDUM 10

Criteria for the Evaluation of Pupil Personnel Services Staff

(Guidance Counselors, School Psychologists, and School Social Workers)*

Knowledge of Theory and Practice

Pupil Personnel Staff shall be able to demonstrate a thorough knowledge of current theories, techniques, strategies, and best practices regarding their respective discipline, with special emphasis on special education classifications and diagnostic categories, to link this knowledge to other disciplines and to be cognizant of local, New York State and National Learning Standards and expectations for students.

Preparation

Pupil Personnel Staff shall be able to demonstrate the ability to plan and prepare meaningful individual and/or group sessions that support New York State and local standards and employ the necessary clinical practices to support student development, progress and achievement, to use appropriate resources and materials, to apply effective intervention strategies, to keep current on the latest research and information as it relates to pedagogical practices, and to follow the best available and most appropriate standard of practice.

Service Delivery

Pupil Personnel Staff shall be able to demonstrate the ability to deliver services that support the individual needs of the diverse learning styles of students, develop and implement both prevention and intervention strategies based upon sound knowledge of psychometric testing results, provide opportunities to promote student competence and participation, engage students in problem solving, decision making, critical thinking, and creativity, encourage active student involvement, foster appropriate teacher/student interaction, and integrate technology, as appropriate.

Management Skills

Pupil Personnel Staff shall be able to demonstrate knowledge of effective management skills to support a learning environment that is conducive to successful student outcomes and supportive of diverse learning needs, to maintain a high rate of student participation, to make effective use of time, case data and materials to develop appropriate recommendations and/or educational interventions, to foster an atmosphere of mutual respect and tolerance, and to model the desirable behaviors of equity, fairness and integrity.

Student Development

Pupil Personnel Staff shall demonstrate an understanding of the intellectual, social, emotional and physical developmental needs of their students and the ability to use this knowledge to adapt, modify and apply developmental^ appropriate prevention and intervention strategies to ensure that all students have the opportunity to succeed.

Student Assessment

Pupil Personnel Staff shall demonstrate the ability to use a variety of psychological, psycho-educational and psycho-social assessment based on accepted psychometric standards as well as appropriate learning standards, to select appropriately from among available measures, to diagnose students' needs, to monitor and assess student progress, and to provide students and parents with regular and timely feedback on their progress.

Report Writing

Pupil Personnel Staff shall demonstrate the ability to prepare written reports and materials that are clear and concise and provide the reader with thorough and useful information that specifically defines needs, problem areas and potential solutions and to translate evaluations into appropriate recommendations or referrals.

Collaboration

Pupil Personnel Staff shall demonstrate the ability to develop positive and effective collaborative relationships with students, parents or caregiver, colleagues, and school district personnel, to share ideas, suggestions and resources with others, and to establish and maintain open channels of communication with all constituent groups for the purpose of fostering a partnership in the educational process and to meet the learning needs of students.

Reflective and Responsive Practice

Pupil Personnel Staff shall demonstrate the ability to reflect critically on their practices and strategies, to apply current educational research and findings to practice, and to effectively assess and appropriately adjust their practice in response to student data on a continuing basis.

Participation in Professional Growth

Pupil Personnel Staff shall demonstrate that they recognize the importance and necessity of continuous professional growth by attending in-service workshops, seminars, and/or graduate classes, and by assisting in material selection, professional readings, school visitations and membership in professional organizations.

Professionalism

Pupil Personnel Staff shall demonstrate professionalism by serving as positive role models for students in appearance, maturity, and use of good professional judgment, respecting the confidentiality of students, parents and colleagues, attending meetings, assignments, classes and school on a regular basis, being punctual, maintaining a generally positive attitude, keeping records as required, following board policy and administrative procedures, being involved with community educational projects as applicable, being involved in school activities, and being prompt and accurate with the preparation of reports or applicable documents.

Participation in Professional Growth

Pupil Personnel Staff shall demonstrate that they recognize the importance and necessity of continuous professional growth by attending in-service workshops, seminars, and/or graduate classes, and by assisting in material selection, professional readings, school visitations and membership in professional organizations.

Professionalism

Pupil Personnel Staff shall demonstrate professionalism by serving as positive role models for students in appearance, maturity, and use of good professional judgment, respecting the confidentiality of students, parents and colleagues, attending meetings, assignments, classes and school on a regular basis, being punctual, maintaining a generally positive attitude, keeping records as required, following board policy and administrative procedures, being involved with community educational projects as applicable, being involved in school activities, and being prompt and accurate with the preparation of reports or applicable documents.

Participation in Professional Growth

Pupil Personnel Staff shall demonstrate that they recognize the importance and necessity of continuous professional growth by attending in-service workshops, seminars, and/or graduate classes, and by assisting in material selection, professional readings, school visitations and membership in professional organizations.

Professionalism

Pupil Personnel Staff shall demonstrate professionalism by serving as positive role models for students in appearance, maturity, and use of good professional judgment, respecting the confidentiality of students, parents and colleagues, attending meetings, assignments, classes and school on a regular basis, being punctual, maintaining a generally positive attitude, keeping records as required, following board policy and administrative procedures, being involved with community educational projects as applicable, being involved in school activities, and being prompt and accurate with the preparation of reports or applicable documents.

*Bellmore Merrick Central School District

ADDENDUM 11

FERPA

Family Educational Rights and Privacy Act (FERPA)

The Family Educational Rights and Privacy Act (FERPA) *(20 U.S.C. § 1232g; 34 CFR Part 99)* is a Federal law that protects the privacy of student education records. The law applies to all schools that receive funds under an applicable program of the ii.S Departrnent *of* Education,

FERPA gives parents certain rights with respect to their children's education records. These rights transfer to trie student when he jr she reaches the age of 18 or attends a school beyond the high school level. Students to whom the rights have transferred are "eligible students.

Parents or eligible students have the right to inspect and review the student's education records maintained by the school. Schools are not required to provide copies of records unless, for reasons such as great distance, it is impossible for parents or eligible students to review the records. Schools may charge a fee for copies,

Parents or eligible students have the right to request that a school correct records which they believe to be inaccurate or misleading. If the school decides not to amend the record, the parent or eligible student then has the right to a formal hearing. After the hearing, if the school still decides not to amend the record, the parent or eligible student has the right to place a statement with the record setting forth his or her view about the contested information

Generally, schools must have written permission from the parent or eligible student in order to release any information. However, FERPA allows schools to disclose those records, without consent, to the following parties or under the following conditions (34 CFR S 99.31):

State and local authorities, within *a* juvenile justice system, pursuant to specific subpoenas.

State law

Schools may disclose, without consent, "directory" information such as a student's name, address, telephone number, date, and place of birth, honors, and awards, and dates of attendance. However, schools must tell parents and eligible students about directory information and allow parents and eligible students a reasonable amount of time to request that the school n.-it disclose directory information about them. Schools must notify parents and eligible students annually of their rights under FERPA. The actual means of notification (special letter, inclusion in a PTA bulletin, student handbook, or newspaper article) is up to the discretion of each school.

ADDENDUM 12
The Kende Trio

CRISTA DANIELA ALEXIS

GUIDING CHILDREN TO BRING JOY TO OTHERS
THROUGH EXCELLENCE
(The Genesis of an Ivy League Student)
By Lisa Kende

"We are what we repeatedly do. Excellence, then, is not an act, but a habit." Aristotle

Until Dr. O'Connell (Doc, for short) retired, we did not fully grasp how much he embodied total excellence in his tireless efforts advocating for each and every student. Thankfully, his retirement provided the time necessary to write this remarkable handbook, a gift to parents, administrators and especially other counselors. More than a guidance counselor, he was a guiding force in our lives, helping us to chart the course that would lead the children from a local public high school to one of the finest universities in the world.

Going to an Ivy League school was never a goal in and of itself; it was the by-product of dedication, remaining focused and putting total energy into achieving excellence in something outside of and in addition to academics. For our girls that something was music. Beginning from as young as 2 years old. Aristotle speaks of excellence as a habit. At age 2, holding a tiny 1/32 sized violin for even a minute or two daily, was the habit that eventually grew into a meaningful skill.

That musical skill was further developed at the Juilliard School, but most of all it grew out of the girls sharing their music in concerts for general audiences. From a very young age, even before their musical skills were very developed, music, in our view, extended well beyond the practice room to the stage, where it could be shared with others to move them to inner peace. At a very young age, the girls and their younger brother (a double bassist) preformed a holiday concert at a cerebral palsy home where the music seemed to calm the uncontrolled moments of even the most handicapped of patients. It provided them with a short reprieve from their physical limitations by allowing their minds to soar where their bodies never could.

From the time the trio was formed in 1997, there were many, many such concerts at nursing homes, schools, libraries, bookstores, universities. Most importantly, in 1999 the girls had the great honor of playing for the late Pope John Paul II at Mass in St. Peter's Basilica and at the general audience. It helped them to realize that music can reveal the divine presence for all who hear it whether they are religious or not. It is just that beautiful and moving. And the combination of music and personal faith is a powerful one, perhaps because it acknowledges that all talent is a gift from God.

In addition to their personal and spiritual growth, music studies gave them the life skills and focus that led to academic excellence, almost by default. Because they wanted to devote several hours daily to building their musical skills, they had no choice but to manage their time efficiently and make every hour count. (A note here that you cannot "make" a child practice, you can only encourage the effort pointing out that while no one relishes the work involved, the results can be very rewarding.) To be honest, not all the girls wanted to practice consistently but their struggle to develop a solid worth ethic at a young age proved to be a valuable life skill. They were committed to developing the musical skill that for nearly 18 years has given them a voice long before they had the words to express themselves. Music continues to reflect whom they are deep inside.

In academics and in music, we realized that a few superb teachers could make the difference. Two high school math and social studies teachers in particular provided the girls with the thinking skills that continue to serve them both at school and in the world. And those very special music teachers who cared enough to develop artistry, not merely technique, were also a key part of the equation. Such teachers realize that mere talent is useless unless it is drawn out and refined much like a sculptor chisels a masterpiece from a simple tree trunk. And the gift of a guidance counselor as insightful, caring, skilled and creative as Dr. O'Connell kept the girls on their path to excellence and eventually guided them to Princeton University, a school where the girls have been able to grow academically, personally and spiritually. Humor was the key weapon in Doc's arsenal and with it he could never ask too much of them.

What has become obvious is that young children and even older ones desire, welcome and need limits and guidance. As the girls' first violin teacher once shared, never allow a child to make a decision that is beyond them. Translation: a 3-year-old child does not decide 'if' they want to practice but simply, "do you want to practice now or 5 minutes from now?" One minute at a time, their tiny squeaks turned into melodious notes and phrases and the best part is that the three sisters came to know one another intimately through their music. When The Kende Trio (www.kendetrio.com) was formed in 1997, the girls were only 10, 12 and 14 years old, but they were old enough to understand that they were a team, later learning how to compensate for one another's strengths and weaknesses. Within their little group, they learned about camaraderie, cooperation, selflessness, all valuable skills that have helped them in all areas of their life. The musical interaction helped them to discover who they were and where their strengths lay and to this day, when they perform, it is as much a conversation between the girls as it is an expression of their deepest emotions.

Ultimately, the quest for excellence in and of itself brings a young person to a higher level of self-confidence and joy at what they have achieved and what they share in bringing joy to others. Taking the time to encourage and help a child develop excellence in anything (whether it be art, sports, dance, chess, music, etc.) is the greatest gift a parent can give to a child. A child who is fulfilled can more easily become a young adult with a mission, namely, to add beauty and grace to our world. There is no such thing as a child who has not been blessed with some special talent or ability. **The more parents are committed to helping their children discover their unique abilities and lead purposeful lives, the happier their and our world will be.**

GLOSSARY OF ACRONYMS

ACT—American College Testing The ACT is one of America's most widely accepted college entrance exams. It assesses high school students' general educational development and their ability to complete college-level work. The multiple-choice tests cover four skill areas: English, mathematics, reading, and science. The Writing Test, measures skills in planning and writing a short essay. www.act.org

A.D.H.D.—Attention Deficit Hyperactivity Disorder

Attention Deficit Hyperactivity Disorder (ADHD) is a condition that becomes apparent in some children in the preschool and early school years. It is hard for these children to control their behavior and/or pay attention. It is estimated that between 3 and 5 percent of children have ADHD, or approximately 2 million children in the United States. This means that in a classroom of 25 to 30 children, it is likely that at least one will have ADHD.

AP—Advanced Placement

College level courses offered to high school students in many subject areas. Successful completion of an AP exam can result in college credit.

A.S.C.A.—American School Counselor Association

ASCA believes in one vision and one voice and works to meet the needs of all professional school counselors, regardless of setting, experience level or needs. With a membership of more than 17,000 school-counseling professionals, ASCA focuses on providing professional development, enhancing school counseling programs and researching effective school counseling practices. ASCA's mission is to represent professional school counselors and to promote professionalism and ethical development. www.schoolcounselor.org

A.S.V.A.B.—Armed Services Vocational Aptitude Battery

This program is designed to help students learn more about themselves and the world of work, and to identify and explore potentially satisfying occupations, and develop an effective strategy to realize their goal. The ASVAB test may be administered to high school juniors and seniors in order to identify areas of strength and avenues of career exploration. www.asvabprogram.com

B.O.C.E.S.—Board of Cooperative Educational Services

BOCES assists districts to operate more efficiently through out-of-district services.

C.P.S.—Child Protective Services

The purpose of the Child Protective Services Act of 1973 is to encourage more complete reporting of child abuse and maltreatment. The law established a Child Protective Service in each county in New York. Each Child Protective Service is required to investigate child abuse and maltreatment reports, to protect children (under 18 years old) from further abuse or maltreatment, and to provide rehabilitative services to children, parents, and other family members involved. www.ocfs.state. nv.us/main/cps/

C.S.E.—Committee on Special Education

The committee is comprised of an administrator, school psychologist, guidance counselor, teaching staff, parent, and additional medical or helping professionals, as well as a parent representative who meet to determine the educational placement and services of the student referred for special education services.

C.S.T.—Child Study Team

The Child Study Team (CST) is a group of specialists employed by the school district to provide consultative, evaluative, and prescriptive services to teachers and parents. The CST, together with school principals and Building Support Committees, makes recommendations for programs and placements, which will best address the needs of students who are experiencing school-related problems.

E.D. /E.A—Early Decision/ Early Action

Early Decision refers to meeting an early college application deadline for admission consideration before the general applicant pool. Acceptance is then binding and all other applications must be withdrawn upon acceptance from the college. Early action is similar however, acceptance in non-binding.

E.D.—Emotionally Disturbed

E.D. is a classification category under which a student may receive Special Education services.

Comprehensive testing, professional evaluation, and parent and teacher observation usually determine this classification.

EFC—Effective Family Contribution

The report back from the Federal Government after filing the FAFSA will indicate the EFC. A number is assigned to the EFC. This number will determine if the student is eligible for a Pell Grant.

E.L.L.—English Language Learner

Any student whose native language is not English.

F.A.F.S.A.—Free Application for Federal Student Aid

The form used by colleges to determine the EFC (Estimated Family Contribution) toward tuition. The colleges use this information to determine students' financial aid allocation. www.fafsa.ed.gov

F.A.P.E.—Free and Appropriate Education

The federal Public Law 102-119, known as the Individuals with Disabilities Education Act, Part B (34 CFR Parts 300 and 301 and Appendix C) mandates that all disabled children receive a free appropriate public education. School districts must provide special education and related services at no cost to the child or her/his parents.

FERPA—The Family Educational Rights and Privacy Act

The Family Educational Rights and Privacy Act (FERPA) (20 U.S.C. -1232g: 34 CFR Part 99) is a Federal law that protects the privacy of student education records. The law applies to all schools that receive funds under an application program of the U.S. Department of Education. (Addendum 11 for a full description.)

FSEOG—Federal Supplemental Educational Opportunity Grant

An FSEOG is for undergraduates with exceptional financial need and students with the lowest EFCs. It gives priority to students who receive Federal Pell Grants. An FSEOG doesn't have to be paid back.

GED—General Educational Diploma

The GED test provides individuals with an opportunity to earn a United States high school credential. By taking and passing a series of five tests, an individual can demonstrate an acquired level of learning that is comparable to that of a United States high school graduate.

G.P.A.—Grade Point Average

The average grade of all coursework taken.

IB—International Baccalaureate

A rigorous, college level program of course work offered to students in eleventh and twelfth grade. (See Addendum 7.)

IEP—Individualized Educational Program

An Individualized Educational Program (IEP) relates to the services specifically designed to meet the unique educational needs of a student with a disability. The program is developed at one or more IEP meetings, and its provisions are detailed in writing in the IEP.

I.Q.—Intelligence Quotient

An Intelligence Quotient indicates a person's mental abilities relative to others of approximately the same age. There are hundreds of specific mental abilities—some can be measured accurately and are reliable predictors of academic success.

L.D.—Learning Disability

L.D. is a disorder that affects the student's ability either to interpret what they see and hear or to link information from different parts of the brain. These limitations may show up in many ways as specific difficulties with spoken and written language, coordination, self-control, or attention. Such difficulties extend to schoolwork and can impede learning to read, to write, to do math, etc. www.ldonline.org

L.O.T.E.- Language Other Than English

N.C.A.A.—National Collegiate Athletic Association www.ncaa.org

N.Y.C.A.—New York Counseling Association
N.Y.C.A. is a strong proactive voice promoting counseling through a collaborative and supportive network for all professional counselors in New York State.

O.H.I.—Other Health Impaired
Other Health Impaired (OHI) describes a student who has been compromised by some genetic disorder, birth defect, or acquired disability other than those described by more specific eligibility criteria, such as Learning Disabled (LD). Such disorders include muscular dystrophy, blindness, deafness, Attention Deficit Disorders (ADDs), and others. This really is a catchall category for students who do not fall into the other, more specific eligibility categories. Students with muscular or skeletal disorders are often eligible for physical therapy to assist them in their mobility and/or occupational therapy to assist them with more fine motor and functional skills, such as grasping a pencil to write.

P.S.A.T. /N.M.S.Q.T.—Preliminary SAT/National Merit Scholarship Qualifying Test
A standardized test that provides first hand practice for the SAT Reasoning Test™. It also provides the opportunity to enter National Merit Scholarship Corporation (NMSC) scholarship programs.

P.P.S.—Pupil Personnel Services
Pupil Personnel Services (PPS) is an integral part of the total education program. The Pupil Personnel Services Department includes school nurses, school counselors, school psychologists, and school social workers. The PPS staff members at each school partner with parents, community, students and other educators to assist in creating an

educational environment conducive to the academic, personal, social and career growth of all students

P.T.A.—Parent-Teacher Association
A not-for-profit association of parents, educators, students, and other citizens who are active in their schools and communities. www.pta.org

R.C.T.—Regents Competency Test

S.A.T.—Scholastic Aptitude Test

S.E.P.T.A.—Special Education Parent Teacher Association
The Special Education PTA (SEPTA) is a parent/teacher organization whose scope and membership represents children in each school district as well as preschool children and children educated out-of-district. SEPTA works closely with the school district, other district PTAs, and regional resources in an effort to develop a better awareness of the unique learning needs of all children. SEPTA is also a member of the National PTA.

SSD—The College Board's abbreviation for Services for Students with Disabilities.

V.E.S.I.D.—Vocational and Educational Services for Individuals with Disabilities The mission of VESID is to promote educational equity and excellence for students with disabilities while ensuring that they receive the rights and protection to which they are entitled. In addition, it assures appropriate continuity between the child and adult services systems; and provides the highest quality vocational rehabilitation and independent living services to all eligible persons as quickly as possible. These services are required to enable these persons to work and live independent, self-directed lives. www.vesid.nvsed.gov

POST SCRIPT

Thank you for purchasing my book. If you enjoyed it and learned something from it, please share the web site with your friends and associates.

www.schoolguidanceservices.com

My message is important and part of the profits, as well, goes to charity. When you are finished with the book, it is important that it gets into the hands of your local superintentent, principal, deans of graduate schools of education, directors of college admissions, members of the board of education or your local PTA. Thanks again.

Additionally, should this handbook be re-edited and you feel that some concept, strategy, technique, etc. should be clarified or amended, send your comments to:
dr.roconnell33@yahoo.com

2084087